Read about

Dorothy Allison
Kitty Tsui
Cherríe Moraga
Joan Nestle
Valerie Taylor
Lee Lynch
Ann Bannon
Katherine V. Forrest
Barbara Grier
Barbara Smith
SDiane Bogus
Lisa Ben
Carol Seajay
Franco
Toni Armstrong Jr.
Lisbet
Jewelle Gomez
Minnie Bruce Pratt
Sarah Schulman
Willyce Kim
Lesléa Newman
Terri de la Peña

About the Author

Kate Brandt has written reviews, interviews, and commentary for such lesbian/gay publications as *Visibilities*, the *Bay Area Reporter*, the *Advocate*, and *HOT WIRE*. In 1990, she was nominated for a Cable Car Award as Outstanding Journalist. Kate Brandt lives in San Francisco with her lover, Paula Lichtenberg.

Happy Endings

Kate Brandt

■

**LESBIAN WRITERS TALK ABOUT
THEIR LIVES AND WORK**

■

www.KCLighthouse.org
The LIKE ME Lighthouse
3909 Main
Kansas City, MO 64111

The Naiad Press, Inc.
1993

Printed in the United States of America on acid-free paper
First Edition

Edited by Yvonne Keller
Cover design by Pat Tong and Bonnie Liss
    (Phoenix Graphics)
Typeset by Sandi Stancil

Library of Congress Cataloging-in-Publication Data

Brandt, Kate.
    Happy endings : lesbian writers talk about their lives and work / by Kate Brandt.
        p.   cm.
    Includes bibliographical references.
    ISBN 1-56280-050-7 : $10.95
    1. Lesbians' writings, American—History and criticism—Theory, etc. 2. American literature—Women authors—History and criticism—Theory, etc. 3. Women and literature—United States—History—20th century. 4. Women authors, American—20th century—Interviews. 5. Lesbians—United States—Interviews. 6. Lesbians in literature. 7. Authorship. I. Title.
PS153.L46B73   1993
810'.9'9206643—dc20
                                                        92-42612
                                                        CIP

To my parents,
who always read whatever I write.

Acknowledgments

The idea for this book took shape when Mark Thompson, senior editor of the *Advocate,* assigned me to interview Dorothy Allison in late 1989, and then painstakingly worked with me to produce an article that would convey the essence of Dorothy's singular personality. I thank Mark for his patience, encouragement, and expertise, and I thank him and his colleagues Gerry Kroll and Bryn Austin for the opportunities to interview and write that they provided to me.

During the three years that it took me to complete this project, I had the support of many people, not least of whom are the twenty-two women whose interviews make up this book. I thank all of them for saying "yes" when I contacted them (despite my lack of reputation and book contract), and for the time they took not only to be interviewed, but also to read their respective chapters and give me feedback before publication.

Many thanks to my publisher, lesbian literary icon Barbara Grier, who agreed to be interviewed for this book and who gave me invaluable advice in putting it together long before either of us knew that she would end up publishing it. Working with Barbara has been an education, an honor, and a delight (even when she called first thing in the morning).

Thanks also to my editor, Yvonne Keller, who brought a discerning eye for detail as well as for the "big picture," a love of and expertise in lesbian literature, and a gently used blue pencil to my manuscript. You were right, Yvonne; it *wasn't* painful!

I thank Joan Nestle, Deborah Edel, and the Lesbian Herstory Archives in New York (LHA), and Bill Walker and the Archives of the Gay and Lesbian Historical Society of Northern California in San Francisco (GLHSNC) for providing invaluable resources for background information on the writers whom I interviewed. Specifically, thanks to Amber Hollibaugh and to LHA for use of the transcript of an interview with Sonny Wainwright (made for Amber's video "Gay Greenwich Village"), which I quote in the introduction and which inspired the title of this book; and thanks to Susan Kennedy of Team San Francisco for leading me to an article on Gay Games III by Kitty Tsui, which I found in the GLHSNC archives and which was a big help in researching Kitty's interview.

Thanks to San Francisco's Old Wives' Tales Bookstore (by way of A. J. Liebling) for the "Freedom of the Press" quotation that titles one of this book's sections.

Thanks to Susan Chasin—who should be in this book—for her good advice and for a chance to write.

Thanks to Denise Alter and Doug Kari for legal advice, and to Denise, Eileen Smiley, Eilleen Clavere and Julie Eseed for looking the other way when I attempted to fit a few chapters in at work.

It is customary to thank people "without whom this book could not have been written." In the case of the following two people, this axiom is literally true.

Writer and historian, good friend, and "honorary lesbian" Eric Garber shared with me his many contacts in the lesbian literary world. When I first was putting together a proposal for this book and deciding whom to interview, Eric would say, "Well, how about this one?" or "How about that one?" and provide me with names and addresses. Many of my query letters to prospective interview subjects began, "Eric Garber gave me your address and said that I might use him as a reference." And once the book was underway, Eric would call regularly to see how I was doing and to cheer me on. His generosity of spirit (and address book) helped to make this book possible.

And what superlatives can I use to thank my lover, best friend, domestic partner, and self-anointed "Editrix," Paula Lichtenberg? She chauffeured me to interviews, bought me a box of floppy disks *and* input a chapter to encourage me to make the big leap to writing on computer, helped with research, read all the interviews and offered editorial suggestions that turned fuzzy phrases into articulate sentences, acted as my secretary when "my" writers called me at our home (where Paula works), came all the way downtown to take me to lunch the day I got my first rejection letter from a publisher, and introduced reality into the conversation whenever I (regularly) decided that the book would *never* be written or published. The joy of producing my first book is enhanced by being able to share it with Paula.

CONTENTS

Introduction

The Beginning of *Happy Endings:*
Lesbian Writing Today

There was a time when "happy endings" were
rarely, if ever, found in books by or about lesbians.
The late New York poet Sonny Wainwright, in an
interview about gay life in the 1940s and 1950s,
commented about books of that period, "You just
didn't have happy endings with women. Couldn't
remember hardly any. And ... that was what I kept
looking for." And Carol Seajay, publisher of *Feminist
Bookstore News,* in speaking of the social forces that
shaped the Women In Print movement in the late
1960s and early 1970s, points out that "there really
were not lesbian novels with happy endings."

But over the past twenty years, lesbian literature

has become confident and self-affirming, thanks to writers such as novelist Lee Lynch, who says of her work, "I wanted positive role models and happy endings. The heck with people who say, 'Oh, [Lee] always writes happy endings!' We need them."

This book of interviews, *Happy Endings: Lesbian Writers Talk About Their Lives and Work,* is the beneficiary of these recent years of lesbian discovery and expression. Lesbian writing, whether newly created, matured by experience, or rediscovered with fresh eyes, became visible and influential in the 1970s and 1980s, when the gay liberation, women's liberation, and Women In Print movements converged to produce writing by, for, and about lesbians: works about our real lives.

Books written by lesbians—novels, memoirs, theoretical analyses—began to be published by the new lesbian-owned presses. Magazines began to be printed that spoke to various aspects of our lives as lesbians: racial, ethnic, class, cultural, sexual. Book-stores that sold only books by women, by lesbians and feminists, opened across the country and around the world. Our past—our herstory—started to be acknowledged, collected, and preserved as archives were established. And even those "unhappy" books of the past (the most positive and realistic of them, anyway) were reissued for new generations of readers.

We had found our voices. And many lesbians, such as the women interviewed in this book, were able to speak to women they had never even met: women in small towns and big cities who read their books and magazines and articles, sat in rapt

2

attention at their readings, and were touched, inspired, motivated, entertained, comforted, and informed by their work.

And so *Happy Endings* is a celebration of lesbian writing and of lesbians who write, a collection of conversations with lesbian novelists, essayists, storytellers, historians, poets, and publishers:

- Dorothy Allison, Kitty Tsui, and Cherríe Moraga honor our class and ethnic upbringings with loving, powerful works that defy the traditions that discourage women from autonomy, from sexuality, and from writing.
- Joan Nestle, Valerie Taylor, and Lee Lynch commemorate our past with their stories of lesbian lives of the 1950s as well as the 1990s—stories of women old and young, butch and femme, experienced and newly out.
- Ann Bannon and Katherine V. Forrest celebrate our lives with bestselling novels that have reassured past and present generations that we were not the only lesbians in the world.
- Barbara Grier, Barbara Smith, and SDiane Bogus dignify the worth of our work with their dedication to "the word." Through their book publishing efforts, many more of our voices can be heard.
- Lisa Ben, Carol Seajay, Franco, Toni Armstrong Jr., and Lisbet strengthen our community by creating and producing

magazines to keep us in touch with each
other and with our ever-changing lesbian
world.

- Jewelle Gomez, Minnie Bruce Pratt, and
  Sarah Schulman inspire and reflect our
  political struggles by the example of their
  activism and their brave and outspoken
  writing.
- Willyce Kim, Lesléa Newman, and Terri de
  la Peña encourage our creative efforts by
  demystifying the process of writing and by
  sharing their expertise and insights into the
  lesbian writer's world.

One book like *Happy Endings* cannot speak with
all of our lesbian writers, nor can it address all
literary genres, all ethnic, racial, and class groups,
all historically important writers and literary
movements, all political points of view—if it could, it
would have to be transported in a truck! But this
inability, in a way, itself exemplifies the growth of
lesbian literature over the last twenty years: more
writers, more books, and more voices than can be
contained in a single volume.

Perhaps more volumes will follow. But for now, I
offer this collection of interviews with great respect
and gratitude for the women who have shared their
thoughts with me, and with appreciation for the
wealth of work that is so readily available to so
many of us lesbians today.

—Kate Brandt
San Francisco, California

I.
LESBIAN WRITERS
TALK ABOUT
THEIR LIVES
AND WORK

"It Was Made Clear to Me That Writing Was Not Something I Was Supposed to Do"

Dorothy Allison

Kitty Tsui

Cherríe Moraga

1.

Dorothy Allison

Telling Tales, Telling Truths

When Dorothy Allison was a girl, she knew what she wanted to be when she grew up. She also knew the future for which her working-class Southern background had prepared her. "I wanted to be a writer," she remembers, but adds, "It was made clear to me that that was not something I was supposed to do. I was supposed to get married and have kids,

---

Interview conducted January 10, 1990. An earlier version of this interview was published as "Trash and Proud of It: Writer Dorothy Allison Stays True to Her Roots" in the *Advocate*, March 13, 1990.

and maybe graduate from high school. I was meant to live in a trailer park and beat my children, that was it. I was supposed to have dozens of them and cripple them, emotionally if not physically."

To say that Allison defied these expectations is to seriously understate the case. The girl who was the "first of all of my cousins to graduate from high school, [and] the *only* one to ever go to college," is today an accomplished and acclaimed writer. She has published a novel, the National Book Award nominee *Bastard Out of Carolina;* a volume of poetry, *The Women Who Hate Me;* and a collection of short stories, *Trash,* which won two of 1988's inaugural Lambda Literary Awards. Allison's work is included in many anthologies of fiction, poetry, and erotica. And when she isn't actually writing, Allison is teaching the basics of writing at classes in San Francisco.

Obviously, Dorothy Allison has come far, both geographically and emotionally, from the South Carolina of her youth. But miles and years don't erase memories, and Allison doesn't believe that they should.

"You are who you grew up to be, for Christ sake," she declares. "You can mature, you can learn about yourself, you can change yourself, but you are shaped by where you came from. And if you reject it, you cut yourself off like a goddamned cloud in the sky; you've got nothing to cling to.

"There was a long period in the 1970s where everybody was changing their names," Allison continues, "and I was horrified. I am a living affront to half my family! My stepfather's family is completely *appalled* that I'm running around wearing his name and doing the things I do and being who I am! Well, tough titty, honey; you're going to have to live with me! I'm not going to give that up; it was damned hard to get to be who I am."

Who Allison is, and was, is revealed in her writing, most pointedly in *Bastard Out of Carolina* and *Trash*. The characters and narratives in both books are based on Allison's own life and family, as she explains in the preface to her short-story collection, *Trash*. Her working-class background inspired the title of that book; "trash" is a word that Allison chose with great deliberation.

"I wanted to have that reference there," she states. "It took me a long time to be proud of being trash, and to be a kind of trash that confronts the label. The success of [certain country singers] and all these folks—honey, you got lots of trash running around being proud of itself! But when I was a kid, to be 'trash'—ooh, honey! And my family is consummate trash. Absolute. We are the people who become mechanics and laundry workers. And to say that there is something good and valuable in that heritage is an act of rebellion, and almost revolutionary."

Trash, the book, rights a literary injustice of which Allison has been aware since childhood. She explains, "I don't believe that the Southern working class that I grew up in is honestly reflected in much fiction in this country. For the most part, it either becomes caricature, or you get that quasi-religious bullshit in which we become saintlike and martyred.

"I'm a compulsive reader. I do read almost everything that comes out. [And] I wasn't there. I was ashamed of the reflections of me that appeared in most literature. The vast majority of people writing fiction in this country *don't know* what it's like to be trash. They have either saccharine notions or caricatures."

Of her own fiction, Allison says, "I don't want to simplify when I write. I want people there with their warts on. I want you to love them even when you hate them."

Allison has succeeded in this objective with her novel, *Bastard Out of Carolina.* The story of young Ruth Anne (Bone) Boatwright, *Bastard* vividly portrays Bone's extended family of mother, step-father, sister, grandmother, aunts and uncles and cousins. Although the book depicts emotional and physical violence, poverty, carelessness, and failure, it also powerfully describes the strength, humor, love, and will to survive that links these family members.

Bastard Out of Carolina is not a lesbian novel, per se, although at the end of the book, one of Bone's aunts gently reveals to her niece that her mysterious romantic past of family legend included a love relationship with another woman. But *Bastard* deftly illustrates a time, place, and class in which survival was a daily struggle, and coming out as a lesbian was not the best means to survive.

It is the background from which Allison eventually claimed her lesbian life, but not until she was older, not until social mores had changed. Allison describes herself as "a transition lesbian. I'm a lesbian who was a dyke before there was a women's movement. I knew I was a dyke when I was a kid; it was very obvious to me and slightly scary.

"[Then] the women's movement came along and

was this enormous burst in my life, which gave me the idea that I could be a different kind of lesbian," Allison recalls. "The way I grew up, lesbians were women who got killed; you know, women who drank themselves to death, women who were objects of ridicule. And I was very determined not to be a victim, not to be poor, not to be stupid, not to get stuck in that life. It became a real conflict for me, being a lesbian and realizing that that made it even harder to get out of the situation I was born to fill.

"Going away to college did not actually rescue me from that; it gave me a recognition that there were things I could do, and it gave me an education. But I was still queer, and all the lesbians that I met were bar dykes. And in the women's movement, bar dykes were anathema!" Allison exclaims with a laugh. "They were so incorrect as to be unmentionable; you were supposed to go out and rescue them and enlighten them. And I didn't want to do that—I just wanted to fuck them, or have them fuck me, whichever. It took me years to do this dance where I get to hang on to loving basically working-class butch women, and at the same time not become what their role expectations would have made me."

Since these working-class "role expectations" did not include being a writer, even higher education, as Allison noted, did not instantly change her ingrained perception of what she could do with her life. "When I was in college, the people who were writers were not me," Allison recalls. "Sensitive young boys became writers. Rich young girls who had had a stay in a mental institution became writers. Those were the people who were my role models as writers.

So I didn't do it; I became a feminist organizer, and went into writing through feminism."

Allison worked on numerous feminist magazines, starting with *Amazing Grace* (which lasted one issue) in 1974. "There was a period in this country, particularly in the mid-1970s, where the lesbian ideal was the lesbian writer," she remembers. "We had all those magazines, and we wrote all that poetry and published each other's poetry religiously, some really fine chapbooks, but enormous numbers of what looked to me [to be] really thin stuff."

However, Allison adds, "A lot of what I've published as a lesbian editor was often not terribly well written, but it was vital, because it was showing each other to ourselves. I did that, by letting my girlfriends read sections of my journals, or writing poetry that I gave to one person. [But] I wanted to write short stories. I wanted to be what I had not found. And it was harder. It took more time."

Allison explains, "I find the work of being a writer really difficult. Sending stories off—submitting them to other people's judgment—I find really difficult. And I've worked on lesbian magazines [since 1974]. But even doing that, I didn't send *my* work off much because it never seemed to me to be either strong enough or nasty enough or worth the trouble.

"Writing to be read is distinct for me from writing for yourself," Allison notes. "And my kind of people do not go to psychologists or therapists. When I got in trouble in college, I went to the counseling office and realized immediately that all I was managing to do was put my scholarship at risk. So journals became for me the only place where I would tell the truth.

"And that is not the same as writing poetry or writing fiction. You can tell the truth to yourself, for yourself, [but] you don't imagine showing that to other people, because when you begin to put stories through that filter in your mind, [and hear] how other people will hear them, you start to tell small lies. And it takes a lot of self-examination to even see where the lies are, because you don't know when you're doing it that you're lying. It took me a long time to figure out that sometimes I was just softening [my stories] so as not to upset people, and sometimes I was making [them] funny just to ease it by. To tell people the absolute honest truth, mostly they don't want to hear it."

Truth and lies, and how and why we use them, are important themes in Allison's fiction. For example, in *Bastard Out of Carolina,* Bone deals with the pain and anger of having to move frequently because of her family's inability to pay rent by inventing a new identity for herself as she starts classes at one of her new schools. And in *Trash,* several characters comment on the lies and stories (and the differences between them) that they tell to themselves and to their friends and lovers.

"Southerners are not raised to tell the truth," Allison declares. "It's rude to inflict the truth on people. The women's movement actually was the first place that there began to be an ethic of confrontation and truth-telling. And it was real hard for me to accept it; like, oh, God, do we have to say it *out loud*?! It took me a long time to believe in it, and I realized that it was the only way I could save myself. Because little lies add up and make big lies."

Allison continues this concern today. As a keynote speaker at the 1992 OutWrite Lesbian and Gay Writers' Conference, Allison preached the gospel of truth-telling to her peers, asking lesbian and gay writers to speak honestly about our lives despite the historical resistance of the mainstream literary establishment to the stories we have to tell.

In the 1990s, however, the mainstream publishing industry has been more accepting of lesbian and gay themes in literature as it has published in increasing numbers the works of our writers. In fact, after publishing her first two books with small feminist presses, Allison signed with Dutton, a major New York publisher, to publish her first novel. But she has no illusions about what it means to be a "mainstream writer."

Allison recounts the time several years ago when she was interviewed "by someone who basically [said], 'Well, now that you have a contract to write a novel for a mainstream press, you're real.' Honey, I've been real all along. They're just beginning to pay attention. And they would not be offering us contracts if they could not sell us, if we had not already developed our audience."

Allison is loyal not only to that audience, but to the lesbian and gay presses that first brought her to readers' attention. "I do not believe that the mainstream presses would be publishing gay and lesbian writers today if our presses had not been doing so for fifteen, twenty years," she asserts. "We have proven that the world does not collapse on itself if a lesbian farts in public and identifies herself as a lesbian. And it's a little more difficult when you have lesbian and gay writers who have published with the lesbian and gay press, and with the alternative small presses, who then go to mainstream presses; we're a little bit more demanding, and we do not do what they want from us so easily."

The self-confidence and success of today's burgeoning community of lesbian and gay writers is a result of several factors, according to Allison. "We have, in the last twenty years, birthed a literary movement, a women's movement, a gay men's movement, and a lesbian movement," she explains. "And they have meshed. Ten years ago, that meshing was unimaginable. The lesbian movement was completely separate from the gay movement.

"The idea that there could be a coalition between lesbian presses and gay presses, and there could be an alliance made between trade presses and small presses, with essentially all of us as queer writers and editors and publishers coming together in some kind of self-identified community—that would not have been possible before," Allison declares.

"And in some ways, I think the reason that it's possible now is not even so much the success of our presses as the difficult times that we've been running into. I mean, this is not the high point of the lesbian and gay literary movement. Our bookstores are in trouble. A lot of our magazines have gone under. A lot of our presses are barely sustaining themselves. We're in an economic crunch. And I think, in some ways, that crunch is what is pushing us together as a community more than our successes. Success is what the mainstream perceives, but in our own community it's not high times, it's hard times, and has been for a while. And it's coalition-building.

"AIDS is part of what I mean by hard times," Allison adds. "It's been devastating, not only to the gay men's community, but to our entire lesbian and gay community. And as a literary movement, we've lost precious people, it's unimaginable. But one of the things that has been an effect of the epidemic has been a renewed commitment to coming out, and to coalition-building, from necessity in large part. I don't think I ever imagined that that would be the effect."

But finding courage and creativity in difficult times is one of Dorothy Allison's strengths. And her writing stands as a document of the power of honesty and will in creating literature that touches the reader's life as well as the writer's.

Works by Dorothy Allison: *Bastard Out of Carolina* (E. P. Dutton, 1992); *Trash* (Firebrand Books, 1988); *The Women Who Hate Me* (Long Haul Press, 1983; updated and reissued by Firebrand Books, 1991)

2.

Kitty Tsui

"I Don't Want to Spend All My Life Fighting"

If you're a reader of lesbian literature, you probably know Kitty Tsui as the author of a collection of poetry and short stories titled *The Words of a Woman Who Breathes Fire* and as a contributor to a number of lesbian anthologies and periodicals. But if your interests run to athletics rather than literature, you might know Tsui as a

Interviews conducted February 10, 1990, and July 30, 1992. An earlier version of this chapter was published as "The Nine Lives of Kitty Tsui" in the *Advocate*, April 10, 1990.

bodybuilder, winner of a bronze medal in the physique competition at Gay Games II and a gold medal in women's pairs physique at Gay Games III.

Each of Tsui's audiences met the other, as well as these two disparate sides of Tsui, at Gay Games III, held in Vancouver, British Columbia, in August 1990, where Tsui not only took part in the physique competition, she also participated in "Words Without Borders," a lesbian/gay writers' gathering, and "Gayla!" a women's cultural festival, both of which were held in conjunction with the Games.

Some people consider it unusual that one woman can excel in such diverse areas; Tsui considers *that* attitude "strange." "I have always done a lot of different kinds of things, and I've been comfortable doing that," she explains. "I bodybuild for health, for the challenge of competing, and because it teaches me discipline. I'm not a disciplined writer, for example."

But, Tsui continues, "I write because our history as Asian women in this country has been distorted; our existence has been denied. And so I write to dispel myths, to dispel stereotypes, and to give my characters voice.

"And I write because I think I was born to write. But I never knew that before. I could never accept the fact that, yes, I can write. I think that I'm just actually coming into my own power. I'm just really now beginning to believe that this is what I'm going to be, this is my mission in life, to write."

This empowerment has been a long time in coming for Tsui, since, as she relates, "I began writing when I was very young." Born in Hong

Kong, she was raised in that city and in England, where her family moved when Tsui was five years old.

"When I went to England, I was put in school there, [but] I did not know the language," Tsui recalls. "So my mother tutored me at home. I was very grateful for that, because it actually gave me a great edge; I started reading the great English classics before I was ten years old. I read *Oliver Twist, Great Expectations, The Count of Monte Cristo, Treasure Island, Black Beauty*. I read a lot.

"Because I grew up the eldest and because I was separated in years from my other siblings, I grew up pretty much alone. And I escaped into books. I loved reading. And I think it was before I was ten years old that I realized that I had the power myself to create stories, and to create adventures. I began writing for publication when I was a teenager in Hong Kong [where her family returned when Tsui was ten years old]. So I started quite a long time ago."

Tsui's work always has been drawn from her life—all aspects of it. "I feel that the strongest things that I write about are things from my own personal experience," she explains. "Even when I was younger, I did not grow up writing stories about blonde, blue-eyed girls. Everything that I've written comes from my experience as an Asian, as a woman, and as a lesbian."

One great influence on Tsui's writing as well as on her life was her grandmother, Kwan Ying Lin, a Chinese opera star, about whom Tsui has written extensively (for example, in her poem "Chinatown

Talking Story" and in her story "Poa Poa Is Living Breathing Light"). "She was the first woman in my life," Tsui explains, "because she raised me. She was, I'm sure, the first woman that I loved. She was very strong and very independent, a very proud woman. One of the projects I'm working on is that I am finally getting down to writing my book about her; it's going to be a novel.

"She was an amazing woman," Tsui continues. "She was a very famous Cantonese opera singer. Chinese opera is very different from Western opera in that it is very much the theater of the people; it wasn't an esoteric art form. The Chinatowns here [in the United States], in the early 1900s, were largely bachelor societies, because there were many laws that prohibited Chinese women from entering. The only kind of entertainment [these societies] had was gambling and the opera. They would recruit stars from China.

"So my grandmother came over here when she was in her twenties. She actually met my grandfather here, in Vancouver; they were married in Oakland. But my grandmother was not a Chinese woman of her time. When she was in her mid-thirties, she left my grandfather, who had three other wives. She took her two daughters and went to live with another woman. This other woman was also an actress, who coincidentally enough used to play male roles on stage.

"So my grandmother had a very exceptional life."

Tsui's grandmother was "actually supportive in a silent way" when Tsui came out as a lesbian at the age of twenty-one, several years after she had moved with her family to San Francisco. "I invited [my grandmother] to come hear me read at San Francisco State University, because she doesn't understand English," Tsui recalls. "Well, she invited my parents. So I thought that I had better come out to my parents before they heard me speak about my lesbianism in a roomful of people. I told my mother, and she started crying and talking about where did she go wrong, and how I'd always wanted to be different and that I was just rebelling and going through a phase.

"That was [in 1973]. And it's never been brought up again. Ever," Tsui states. "When [*The Words of a Woman Who Breathes Fire*] came out in 1983, it got reviewed in an Asian community newspaper. My aunt called my mother and told her that I had a book out. So my mother asked me for the book, which talks about, among other things, my being a lesbian, my having been an alcoholic. And again it was the same thing; I gave her the book and it was like it never happened. She never asked me about it again, she never talked about it, she never discussed it, ever again. It's one of those many things that get swept under the rug."

Coming out as an Asian lesbian, Tsui felt isolated from both her worlds. Although as a teenager she worked in San Francisco's Chinatown as a drug counselor and a tutor, she recalls, "When I came out, I felt very odd and very much like a sore thumb because the climate was very heterosexual. So I basically withdrew from the Asian community and tried to find a lesbian community that I could be part of."

But, Tsui adds, "When I first came out, in the mid-1970s, there was no visible lesbian community. There weren't a lot of books, certainly no role models that I could find. I went to bars, and I felt very strange, very different. I saw many white people; I thought I was the only Asian lesbian in the world. It was very lonely.

"I was fortunate in that in the first six months of my coming out, I met another Chinese woman, who became my first lover. And so I created a community with her and a group of her friends, who were all Chinese lesbians from Hong Kong. But I think it was quite a long time before I felt like there was a lesbian community into which I fit."

It was as a writer that Tsui began to find her place. "In the early 1970s, I met a group of women of color who were [active as writers and artists]. I started doing a lot of readings, and having my work published."

In 1979, Tsui and five other Chinese American women realized "that there was a distinct lack of representation by Chinese American women on the literary scene," Tsui continues. "So we got together to do a poetry reading, and there was a great response; I think there were three hundred people who came to our reading. We realized that there was a great need for our voices."

As a result, the women began working as a group they called Unbound Feet. "We formed to perform our work—we thought we'd do it maybe twice a year—and after the first performance, we were in so much demand that we ended up doing quite a few readings and writing workshops, for about a year and a half.

"[Then] we realized that we had two different goals. Three of us felt it was really important that our art and our politics were intertwined and that we couldn't separate them. The other three felt more like our work should be creative, and that we shouldn't really talk about politics. And that was a big difference.

"So the group split. The three of us who wanted to pursue our writing along with our politics formed into Unbound Feet Three, and that was myself, Nellie Wong, and Merle Woo. Unfortunately, the other three, even though they didn't want to go on any longer, felt we shouldn't go on with the name. So we experienced a year of turmoil where they tried to sue us; it was a lot of unpleasantness, letters going back and forth, letters to the gay press; they would picket our readings. We just wanted to go on with our work!"

Tsui did "go on," becoming a writer of renown in the lesbian, feminist, and Asian communities. Still, her traditional Chinese background did not always make it easy for her to write about herself. "I come from a culture and a tradition that treats women as second-class citizens," Tsui points out. "My grandmother escaped having her feet bound because she was poor, but she was from that generation where women had their feet bound and their marriages arranged; they had no rights."

Of her own girlhood, Tsui recalls, "I grew up in Hong Kong where I would hear people saying to their daughters when they were bad, 'Oh, you dead girl.' We were called 'dead girls.' We weren't even called 'brats' or 'naughty children,' we were called 'dead people,' 'dead girls.'

"So I feel like it really takes a lot of self-esteem and self-motivation combined with the creativity that we have in order to say to yourself, 'Yes, I'm a writer and this is what I'm going to do.' For me, I feel like all these years I have done my writing 'on the side.' I've always done it when I have an editor call me saying, 'Where's your stuff?' or I have a publisher calling me saying, 'I want this from you.' That was the only time I ever really wrote. So I never believed in myself as a writer. I would just write 'on the side.' Until just recently."

Asked what made the difference in her perception of herself as a writer, Tsui responds, "Anger. I look at anthologies, I go to writers' conferences, and I see that Asian American writers are still invisible. When people think of inclusion, they think mainly about Black and white, and possibly Hispanic, and *possibly* Native American. Asian Americans are still invisible. I feel like we are the ones who have to speak out, we are the ones who have to say, 'Hey, we're here, we're not invisible, we demand to be heard.'

"It's that kind of anger that really pushes me to write, to work, to keep struggling, to keep fighting for a voice and for recognition. I've been writing for quite a long time; I've been very active in the gay and lesbian community, and the arts community, for practically twenty years. There's a great deal of frustration when you look in an anthology and you're not included—and I'm not saying 'me,' I'm saying 'we.' *We* are not included.

"I think about all these years of fighting and struggling and screaming to be heard and trying to make yourself visible, and [that] there still [isn't] any *hint* of visibility is frightening. I don't want to spend all my life fighting. I want to do some writing! I don't want to be writing letters to the editor. I don't want to be calling publishers on their lack of inclusion. I've spent so much of my life doing this. I'm tired! I'm angry! I want to spend my time writing, doing my work.

"It's a sad state," Tsui concludes. "As Asian women, we haven't been encouraged to write, to express ourselves. It's much easier for straight Asian women who have books that really exoticize a lot of aspects of Chinese American life, specifically Maxine Hong Kingston and, in a small way, Amy Tan. It's much easier for them to write a book that appeals to the mainstream. We [Asian lesbians] are writing about a part of our lives that the Asian community doesn't want to look at, doesn't want to acknowledge."

But Kitty Tsui is making sure that the Asian community, as well as the lesbian and literary communities, acknowledge her and her work. In addition to the novel about her grandmother's life, Tsui's other current projects include a second book of poetry and fiction, this one to be called *Nice Chinese Girls Don't,* as well as a collection of erotica to be titled *Breathless.*

And she still is bodybuilding, making plans to participate in Gay Games IV in 1994. While the challenges of bodybuilding differ from those of writing, the rewards do, as well. For as Tsui herself admits, with a rueful laugh, speaking of her stint in

Gay Games II, "I took the bronze medal in the lightweight women's category in physique, and got more recognition for my sixty seconds on stage than in my fifteen years of writing!"

Work by Kitty Tsui: *The Words of a Woman Who Breathes Fire* (Spinsters, Ink, 1983)

3.

Cherríe Moraga

A Question of Identity

"The combination of my lesbianism and my Chicanismo, my Chicano identity, are fundamental to everything I've written. They both are power sources for me; they drive me to write." Playwright, poet, essayist, editor, teacher, activist: Cherríe Moraga's many identities as an artist are rooted in her primary identity as a Chicana lesbian—an identity that had to be revealed and reconciled within herself before it could "drive" her writing.

"I wrote some in college, very poorly, largely

Interview conducted April 3, 1991.

because I was writing with a secret," Moraga recalls about her coming-out process. "I always wanted to write about lesbianism, but couldn't honestly deal with the subject. So what came out were these very sort of homophobic, horrible stories that touched the subject and got scared.

"I didn't really start writing seriously until I was out of college," Moraga continues. "By then I had come out as a lesbian and I didn't have to keep things secret. This relieved the great burden in me. Suddenly I was able to write in a way that was full-bodied. Also, I began to be a feminist, and there was that context in which to write. So I started writing with real seriousness."

But it was the influence of her Chicano culture that, in Moraga's words, "just exploded my writing. Becoming conscious of the impact that my culture had on the formation of my sexuality, my self, my womanhood, was very, very significant to me. It had the same impact that the relief of the revelation of my own lesbianism had on my writing. I think that, probably more than anything, trying to unravel what I had been told was a contradiction in those two identities [Chicana and lesbian] existing in the same person is what continues to propel me to write."

Of her early influences, Moraga admits, "I was a terrible reader, hated to read, was a very slow reader, all through grade school. And then in high school, I was a much better talker than I was a reader—you know, I could just kind of talk my way through stuff; I was a 'smooth talker.' So my relationship to reading and writing was pretty removed.

"For me to write was out of the pure desire to

express myself. When I was very young, I drew; when I was a little bit older, I played the trumpet—any way in which I could express myself. And so writing was just about expression; there was no expectation attached to it. The value around education was very high in my family, and that value had to do with the fact of securing a decent *job*, in which one didn't have to work factory and you could dress nice every day. If you could read and write well, then you were secured of a decent living. If we wanted to go to college, they encouraged us, but it wasn't an expectation."

Therefore, as Moraga points out, "The difficulty for me in writing, particularly in my younger years, [was] that it wasn't *going* to make a living. What was valued by my family were those professions, those occupations, that would secure you a good living. I taught high school for a couple of years, and everybody was happy with me! You know, I had a *real* job, I had credit, I had arrived! I had accomplished what, in my family—and I say this with respect—for them, was a great achievement; to become college-educated and to have a profession was an incredible achievement.

"So the whole notion of *art*, writing for art's sake, or for political change or for simple self-expression, those are things that just emerged out of my own spirit, my own hunger as a human being. [Now] I wake up every morning marveling at the fact that I have managed to make a living in any way remotely related to my writing. The fact that I publish and that people pay me to read my work remains sort of miraculous, in terms of my point of reference."

In her groundbreaking book of autobiographical

essays, *Loving in the War Years: Lo Que Nunca Pasó Por Sus Labios,* Moraga wrote of how her writing separated her from her family, yet also brought her closer to them. She explains, "When I'm writing and I'm writing well, I know that I'm trying to write out of a place of love and compassion, for my characters, for myself, for all of those who have influenced me. Particularly in the last five years, I primarily have been writing theater, and all of it is basically connected to Chicano culture and resides in the Chicano context, Chicano family. So I feel that the act of writing brings me closer to my family by virtue of the fact that it continues to open me up more and more to the significance of that way of viewing the world.

"The separation that I feel has to do with the fact that the act of writing itself, and particularly as a lesbian and the way I deal with issues of sexuality, is so dangerous on some level, and so private, and so unheard of—there's no context to really understand it in relation to my family," Moraga explains. "But the act of writing itself opens my heart to [my family], and the ways in which I have been affected by them, both positively and negatively, and it also forgives them. So on that level, it makes me more able to connect with them in the real world. But, of course, the writing process itself and the kind of lifestyle that evokes—and also because I write so much about lesbianism and sexuality—there's a separation that has to happen, because there's not a lot of understanding about *why* I have to write about those kinds of things."

If there is a lack of understanding from the Chicano culture about lesbianism, there is a similar lack of understanding within the white lesbian culture about being Chicana, and both have erected barriers for the Chicana lesbian writer. "I feel like we've barely begun to scratch the surface," Moraga states. "We [Chicana lesbians] only really began to publish seriously beginning in the 1980s, so we have barely a decade of publishing, and the writers [who] have published more than one book of any significance, in terms of sales, we can count on one hand. Even the Chicanas who aren't out as lesbians, but are dealing specifically with issues of sexuality—you know, it remains so taboo. It remains taboo within the Chicano context. And it remains taboo in a mainstream context. Nobody is allowing us to be all of those things [Chicana, lesbian, sexual] at once together.

"I feel like there has been some progress," Moraga adds, "and things have changed, but I remain ever awed by how forbidden it still is for us just to open our mouths and to talk very specifically about the ways in which both we have been damaged and also the joy and the pleasure and the affirmation of being our 'multiple identities'—which is one identity; we're just made to think of it as multiple." Moraga's recent concentration on theater work has reinforced these impressions. "I am constantly reminded by how resistant the people in positions of producing you are to looking at themes that are really Chicano themes, that really deal with the complexity of being both female and a woman of color at the same time," she notes. "You can tell this from the racist and sexist reviews of my plays by white male critics."

But Moraga insists on doing it. "In [my] play

Heroes and Saints, there's a character who's just a head. She represents a lot of things to me. At one point, she's saying to a priest who's befriended her that she doesn't have a body, that she's been denied one, and when she explains [how] she misses her body, [how] she just hungers for her body—to me, she's the Mexican woman; she's the Chicana who has not been allowed to wholly inhabit herself. And when we *dare* to have a brown woman be sexual and be the subject of our work, it meets with great resistance. It's acceptable to create a stereotypical image of the Chicana or to use her in some kind of tokenistic way, put her in some kind of category of behavior, like 'the suffering mother' or 'the virgin' or whatever. But if you write about what we're *really* like in all our complexities, no one wants to hear."

However, Moraga sees signs of change in the work of younger Chicana lesbians. "I look forward to what a generation of women coming up are going to do," she says. "For example, there's an anthology [*Chicana Lesbians: The Girls Our Mothers Warned Us About,* edited by Carla Trujillo, 1991] by Third Woman Press and many of the contributors are in their early twenties. They're writing stuff that—I mean, when I was in my early twenties, I could barely even imagine! And so that gives me hope; that gives me a lot of hope. But they have role models! They have somebody to read. We didn't have anybody to read twenty years ago."

Moraga and her contemporaries dealt with this lack of work by lesbians and feminists of color by producing their own, most notably the milestone anthology *This Bridge Called My Back: Writings by Radical Women of Color,* which Moraga edited with

Gloria Anzaldúa. Moraga reflects that "It's funny, because when *Bridge* came out [in 1981], I got a lot of attention very very quickly, and I wasn't at all prepared. I had published two poems in my life before that book, and then suddenly this book is selling like hotcakes. It really confused me, because I didn't feel like a spokesperson, which the book put me in the position of being. I wasn't really ready for all the attention *and* the responsibility.

"After about a year or more of doing a lot of public appearances, promoting *Bridge,* I finished *Loving in the War Years,* but nobody paid much attention," Moraga recalls. "Although there's always been consistent women-of-color response to *Bridge,* the strong sales and the university readings usually occurred through white feminist networks. Suddenly, when I was writing about really being Chicana and not within the larger 'women-of-color framework,' it wasn't that interesting; it wasn't that fashionable.

"In 1983, [when *Loving* was published]" Moraga explains, "there was little precedent for white feminists to look at racism or cultural diversity through the eyes of a Chicana. I say this, understanding that racism in this country is viewed very much on a Black/white kind of spectrum, and so Black women have always been more interesting to white women, whose 'interest' stems from their own racist guilt and fear toward African American women and possibly a shared 'Americanism,' but has rendered most other women-of-color groups largely invisible. When *Loving* came out, I started to really *see* that.

"Around the same time, I also felt like I needed to really do some organizing, and that's when I [co-founded] Kitchen Table: Women of Color Press, and I started to do women-of-color organizing around violence against women. On some level, I almost had to live up to in practice what *Bridge* was [propounding] on paper.

"Then I really got back to the business of being a writer. I came back out to California, I stopped doing any speaking gigs for a number of years—I just got into the work of being a writer. Recently, I've come up from underground, or out of hiding, and at the same time, I have gotten various kinds of recognition. The thing that's been really really good about it for me is that it feels solid! It feels like I've really done the work."

Moraga adds, "It's very important that you get affirmation, so that you'll continue to do the work. Because I feel that equally, I encounter obstacles; equally, I encounter rejection; equally, I encounter people who basically let me know that, by virtue of [my] being a Chicana lesbian, they're not interested in me, that I'm 'too much,' in the wrong ways. And so, to get expressions of affirmation on the basis of my work is really what [I] need to balance the picture."

What does Moraga think would have to happen to make circumstances better for writers such as herself? "What has to change is that writers, Chicana lesbians, have to write within a political context," she asserts. "They have to write within a social movement. They have to be activists. And by that, I don't mean that they should be out on the streets organizing, necessarily. But they have to see themselves as writing in order to save the planet. Just because you're published doesn't make that big a difference to the world. The token writer doesn't change things. It's *what* you're saying that counts.

"So to me, identity in and of itself will not save us. If you've got Chicanas writing and they just want to be assimilated into the mainstream with a little Chicana lesbian twist, it doesn't make any difference. But if their identity forces them to raise the issues that nobody wants to deal with, which have to do with race and class and sex and sexuality, then there's hope."

Of her own work, Moraga says, "I feel like I write within a community; and right now, I *don't* identify that as lesbians. I identify now much more in terms of people of color and specifically Chicanos and Latinos, and a kind of Latin American voice. I feel that really strongly. I consider myself somebody who will always be writing within a political framework; that's why I call myself both a Chicana and a lesbian writer. Otherwise, I could be a 'Hispanic' who writes about sexuality. To claim myself as a lesbian and claim myself as Chicana is a political statement. I'm not Mexican American, I'm Chicana. And as 'dyke' was a derogatory word reclaimed by lesbians as a statement of affirmation and resistance, so is the term 'Chicano.' We are people of Indian blood. We are not hyphenated Americans. So if I'm saying I'm Chicana and I'm a dyke, then I'm writing in a context in which, I'm trying to shape a world in which, one can be free in both of those areas."

One result of being a proud, "out" Chicana dyke is that Moraga often finds herself being courted specifically for her ethnic and sexual identity—for example, in literary anthologies. "I'm often the one Latina or Chicana in the collection," she acknowledges, "and for the most part, I try to ensure that that doesn't happen. But I think about the Chicana who's going to find the book, and that she'll at least read me. And not that I represent her, but that maybe something of what I have to say will speak to her, and she won't be so alone somewhere out there.

"But tokenism—that's not my problem," Moraga concludes. "The people who tokenize you, that's their problem. I just go on with my work."

Works by Cherríe Moraga: *Loving in the War Years: Lo Que Nunca Pasó Por Sus Labios* (South End Press, 1983); *Giving Up the Ghost* (West End Press, 1986); *This Bridge Called My Back: Writings by Radical Women of Color*, co-edited with Gloria Anzaldúa (Persephone Press, 1981; republished by Kitchen Table: Women of Color Press, 1983)

Bridging Generations

Joan Nestle
Valerie Taylor
Lee Lynch

4.

Joan Nestle

"The Whole World Changed"

Joan Nestle came out as a lesbian—a
self-identified femme—in the late 1950s, when she
was a teenager. As lesbian life was changed by the
advent of the gay and women's liberation movements
in the 1960s and 1970s, Nestle found herself
becoming a chronicler and caretaker of the "old days"
of lesbianism and its evolution over four decades,
both through her own writing and through her work
with the nationally renowned Lesbian Herstory
Archives (LHA) in New York City.

Interview conducted March 19, 1991.

LHA had its beginnings in 1973, in a group founded "to set up an organization to represent lesbian and gay students and teachers in the City University [of New York]," Nestle explains. "We started talking about the fact that several of us [women] had come out before the 1970s, that there had been a lesbian culture before the 1970s, but that it seemed to have gotten lost. And we were concerned that, even though the seventies were the heyday of lesbian publishing, this could happen again.

"So we came up with the idea to see if the community would be interested in something called the Lesbian Archives. We did up a letter and sent it to all the known lesbian organizations and newspapers at that time. Out of the [original] group, twenty-five women started to meet about this thing called the Lesbian Herstory Archives. Over the months, the group scattered. Basically, Deborah Edel [Nestle's then-lover] and I were the ones who said we would commit our lives to [LHA]. Everybody else moved to different places, and couples broke up. [So,] in 1974, [LHA] took up house in Deb's and my apartment, and it has been in this apartment ever since."

While many political activists sacrifice their private lives for their work, few literally live with their cause, as Nestle has done for more than seventeen years. Then in 1992, LHA's successful fundraising campaign allowed the group to buy a building in the Park Slope section of Brooklyn, New York. LHA's new home will house the Archives and serve as a lesbian cultural center. But although the purchase will return Nestle's apartment to her, she confesses with a laugh that "the Archives hides [the fact] that I have no furniture in here!"

Reflecting on the soon-to-be-ending years during which she shared her home with the Archives, Nestle admits, "I'll really miss it." She explains, "I have a chronic illness, and the Archives kept me going. There were weeks, months, when I could do nothing but clip articles, but I felt like I was doing important work. It brought people to me; it brought women to me. Sometimes when I can't sleep, still, I just walk the room and it gives me such life."

The Archives stayed in Nestle's Upper West Side apartment for so many years because "we knew that we could never do fundraising in the kind of way we'd have to do it if we had to pay rent. And I'm a socialist; this is a very large apartment, and I couldn't see just living here myself, or with my lover. But it was just the perfect space for the Archives.

"I think when we started the Archives these fifteen, almost twenty years ago, we said that we would become our community's memory. But we were young, and didn't think of our own dying; and now that's coming true. And the Archives has grown much too big for this apartment; I've grown older; Deb has moved out; and it's time for the Archives to evolve to another level."

While Nestle says of living with the Archives, "I would never have wanted to exchange it for anything," she also notes that "there are books I've never written because of the Archives. I help other women do their research, so I never really get time to do mine. I don't mean that to sound like 'Oh, poor me,' but because I live with the Archives all the time, I can see the work it needs all the time, so it keeps me sometimes from having a peace of mind that one would need to do some other kinds of creative work. But, in the other sense, it has fed every creative work I've done. I use the voices in these rooms for all my writing."

Some of these voices are those of the working-class lesbians that Nestle met in the lesbian bars of the 1950s. In her writing, Nestle relates the path that she and others took in traveling from the bar world of the McCarthy years to the new post-Stonewall era of lesbian-feminism. It was a road with few signposts.

"In New York, we had CR [consciousness-raising] groups that grew out of the Gay Activist Alliance," Nestle recalls. "What I quickly learned was that class was an issue, but we *never* talked about it. I learned, basically, that the old lesbian ways that had gotten me to that little group of chairs pulled together were not discussable. We were in such a minority—old-time lesbians who had crossed over—that we really passed in a way. We learned a new language [but] we didn't know what we were losing. We didn't know what we were bartering away for the wonderful woman-safety of feminism.

"And it's taken a lot of years to sort that out. Lesbianism was made to feel like a second-class experience, or *third*-class experience, without feminism. What it really was, was a new generation of women staking out political territory, who didn't have their roots in the bars, who didn't have their roots in being 'queer,' but who had their roots in a women's liberation movement. I think the really exciting time was in the late seventies, early eighties, when we could start bringing all the sides together."

Nestle describes those years of transition and change—"what I call the Queer Fifties, and the Lesbian Sixties, and the Feminist Seventies"—as "absolutely necessary; I wouldn't have wanted one without the other." Similarly, despite the diversity of today's generation of lesbians, Nestle says, "I always hold out that, yes, there is a community. I think it's perhaps more [accurate] to say it's parallel communities that come together, [for example,] for political demonstrations that cut across lines."

Nestle sees our literature as one lifeline available to strengthen our sense of community. "Lesbian writing plays a tremendous survival role and culture communication role for the lesbian reader," she declares. "I think, because so many of us lived secret lives in small towns across the country, that The Book—The Lesbian in The Book—was the open field, you know? It was the place where the doors and windows opened. It was of incredible importance to have the work available. Now, in this time, I think it's revolutionary: the amount of lesbian writing and the variety of it. I think it's one of the pillars of our political movement, and of our eventual survival as a community."

Does Nestle therefore think that these books still are necessary to lesbians in the 1990s? Are we, in fact, a literate community? "I know, from teaching writing, how so many of my kids are tuned in to the non-print media. But the non-print media does not have what our lesbian writers are giving," Nestle responds. "It doesn't give all the fullness of life to someone who is leading a restricted life. There aren't that many lesbian movies and mixed-media things.

"I think we're a literate community because we're desperate for voices to reach us. And that's what these written works are; they make the contact that could be missing from one's day. And for someone who is trying to survive, they're the secret cache of survival that you can carry around. So I think, yes, we're literate because we need the liberation of the pages."

Sometimes, though, that liberation is constrained by censorship, from both within and without. Nestle herself experienced censorship as well as censure from segments of the lesbian community during the 1980s in reaction to her explicit, sex-positive essays and short stories.

But today Nestle feels that these attacks have become less widespread and less personal. She says, "I think many of the women who turned into sex thought-police were truly concerned about violence against women, and had their own horrible experiences: a very deeply experienced vulnerability and a frustration with how to make this culture responsive to the well-being of women. Those are their best motives."

Nestle continues, "[But] I think they took the wrong way. I think that what came in there was perhaps a lack of exposure to other sexual energies, to other sexual ways of being. And there were some women who just are fervent, who are arrogant in their sense that they think they know how to protect women. I'm thinking of women who make careers out of stimulating an anger we all feel, and that anger and that pain is where they've decided to make their culture. And I've decided to make a culture out of another side of it, which is sexual exploration and celebration. And I think both sides are needed."

But Nestle adds, "I felt the censorship coming from their side, not from my side. Andrea Dworkin's books are all in the Archives. I would *never* say, 'Keep her books off the shelf.' But they would say, 'Keep Joan's books off the shelves.'"

Mainstream censorship has been less of a problem for Nestle because, she explains, "I seldom write, in a conscious way, for the outside, for the other world. The fact that they're there doesn't ever stop me from doing anything, because I never expect them to pay any attention to me, and I never ask them for money.

"But the censorship within our community—because that's where I have my life as a writer—that's a harder one for me. Because of my fear of my community, my fear that—I don't ever want to hurt a woman through my writing. I *don't* want to add to the victimization of women.

"There are issues I haven't explored in my writing because I'm afraid of losing my community if I do. So my community is my reason to write. I'm not important enough a writer to be directly affected by straight censorship, though I speak against it all the time. The censors that get to me are my community and myself."

When Nestle is not actually writing, she may be found collecting and editing other women's work. *Women on Women,* the short-story anthology that she co-edited with Naomi Holoch, was a 1990 Lambda

Literary Award winner. And Nestle describes her newest anthology, *The Persistent Desire: A Femme/Butch Reader*, as "a very controversial book—talk about peer censorship!" But this collection of writings about butch/femme identity also is, for Nestle, "something I want to give my world."

Nestle recalls, "When I wrote [about butch/femme relationships] in 1981, I was very careful, and I was still trying to placate lesbian-feminist gods. I didn't take the risks I should have taken. In this book, all the risks are there. There are the voices of stone butches, and passing women, and flamboyant femmes, saying things that [are] very confronting, in some ways, to some prevailing languages that we use. This [book] is the monument that I want to have a hand in creating to this historical community, and as sort of a legacy to present-day women who love this way, the butch/femme way."

"Giving something to my world" and "creating a monument" are very vital concepts to Nestle. For her, the turning point when lesbians and gay men finally were able to say that we do indeed have a history "is both a personal journey and a communal one. But certainly, the advent of the grassroots lesbian and gay history projects was a turning point for me.

"Before then, we collected, we had the Archives—but I'm not a trained historian. [Then I met historians] Jonathan Ned Katz, and John D'Emilio, and Liz Kennedy and Madeline Davis, and Allan Bérubé. We were all working together, and that was a real turning point: [to realize] that those women I knew in the bars were history. When I saw that, then there was no stopping; then, the whole world changed."

But that perspective was not yet available to Nestle in the working-class lesbian bars of the 1950s. What *was* the future that she envisioned at that time? "I can't really say that I envisioned what exists now, the fullness of our institutions and our political public faces," Nestle reflects. "But I could envision a time when I wouldn't believe that I was that criminal and that shameful human being [that I was told I was]. That there would be a time when I could be a full person—that's what I could envision. Because I knew I *was* a full person."

It's in part because Joan Nestle and other brave lesbians knew thirty years ago, in spite of what society was telling them, that they were not "criminals" or "shameful human beings," that those of us who came out in later years can take for granted our pride in being lesbians. And it's because Nestle has so lovingly acted as a medium for all those silenced voices of years past, through the Lesbian Herstory Archives and through her books, that those of us who might have thought we were the only lesbians in the world know that we have a history.

Works by Joan Nestle: *A Restricted Country* (Firebrand Books, 1987); *Women on Women,* co-edited with Naomi Holoch (Plume, 1990); *The Persistent Desire: A Femme/Butch Reader* (Alyson Publications, 1992)

5.

Valerie Taylor

Writing Since the 1950s and Still Going Strong

Mention Valerie Taylor's name to a lesbian reader whose library (or interest) predates gay liberation, and one response that you might provoke is "She's a 'pulp' writer," because of Taylor's paperback novels such as *Whisper Their Love* and *The Girls in 3-B* (1957 and 1959; both now out of print). But ask Taylor *her* opinion of that label, and she declares, "I rather resent being thought of as a pulp novelist."

Interview conducted March 30, 1991.

To Taylor, a pulp novel is "a little more melodramatic than real life, the characters not being as fully developed as they are in a really good book." And that definition contradicts Taylor's reason for writing lesbian fiction in the first place: "I thought that we should have some books about lesbians who acted like human beings."

Taylor "began writing when I was very young—romantic stories of boarding school life. And I began writing lesbian stories in the late 1950s partly because I wanted to get some money, of course—had I known how little money is in it, I might have tried something else—but there's been a great deal of satisfaction in it.

"At that time, there was a great upsurge of lesbian fiction, and it was very trashy. Most of it was written by men under romantic-sounding female names. So I thought it would be nice to write some stories about people who acted human, who had problems, and families, and allergies, and jobs, and so on. Those [other] early books were full of people who did nothing but leap in and out of beds, and stayed out long enough to send the sheets to the laundry."

Taylor's first lesbian novel was called *Whisper Their Love*—"a disgusting title," according to Taylor— one that was chosen by her publisher. "I called it *The Heart Takes Many Paths*, and I started it with an old Arabic proverb, 'The heart takes many paths in search of love'—I was the old Arab, of course, who invented the proverb—but [the publisher] changed it, and called it *Whisper Their Love*. That was the style at that time."

In another convention of the time, the book "had

a little [blurb] by a 'reputed psychologist'—I figure
he was probably the office boy—" Taylor notes wryly,
"saying, in effect, 'Parents, buy this book; it will
keep your daughters from succumbing to the
temptations of lesbianism.'" The protagonist of
Whisper Their Love did "succumb to the temptations," but only briefly, much to the dismay of some
of Taylor's readers. "I was given a great deal of
abuse from people writing in later, because the girl
ended up in a pure love with a man," Taylor admits.
"That was almost required [at that time]; either she
[killed] herself, like the woman in [Lillian Hellman's
play] *The Children's Hour*, or she fell in love with a
man."

But expectations for lesbian novels changed as
the market changed. Taylor explains, "There were
people who were interested in something besides
love-'em-and-leave-'em stories, and who wanted to
read something a little more realistic. And people
came along like Ann Bannon, for example, and
[publishers] revived some of the oldies like Gale
Wilhelm. The audience was *there*. The readership
was *there*. And then the *Ladder* popped up during
that time and published people's short stories."

During this time (the early 1960s), Taylor
continued to write lesbian fiction. Her novels of this
period followed three characters through what
became a related series of books. "I wrote a book
called *Stranger on Lesbos* [1960; now out of print],"
Taylor recounts, "about this middle-class woman
[Frances] who discovers she's a lesbian. Then, I
wrote a book called *A World Without Men* [1963],
which is basically about a woman named Kate who
is an alcoholic and a lesbian, and Kate becomes

involved with Erika Frohmann. Then, I did *Return to Lesbos* [1963], in which Frances and Erika get together.

"And then somebody at [my publisher] Midwood Tower, which was struggling to stay alive, said, 'Why don't you do a book about Erika as a teenager, when she first became a lesbian?' Teenage books were very popular then. So I did *Journey to Fulfillment* [1964], because by this time, I had filled in, in my own mind, all of Erika's back history."

Three of these books were reprinted in the 1980s. But although Frances was the focus of the first and last books of the original series, the three reissued volumes were reprinted as "The Erika Frohmann Series," with *Journey to Fulfillment,* the story of Erika's early years, as the first book, followed by *A World Without Men* and *Return to Lesbos.*

Erika first appeared in Taylor's books as Kate's lover in *A World Without Men.* But when Taylor decided to continue Erika's story, she "killed off" Kate and brought back Frances as Erika's lover. "I was sort of entranced with Erika. I know every little detail about her. Maybe I knew her in some other life—assuming we do get 'recycled.' Makes more sense than anything else," Taylor adds drolly.

"But I was through with Kate when I was through with that one book. It was like a mystery, and once you solved the puzzle, it wasn't very interesting. I *liked* Kate, and I was very sorry for Kate, but I just was through with her. It just turned out I wasn't through with Erika; I didn't know that at the time."

Taylor certainly was not through with Erika, as it turned out, since she and Frances reappeared over twenty years later in a sequel to the series titled *Ripening*, published in 1988. "It isn't as good a book as the others, I think," Taylor admits, "but it sort of rounds off the series."

But what is most remarkable about *Ripening* is its place in Valerie Taylor's *second* career as a lesbian writer. After spending most of the 1960s "working all day and writing 'confession' stories [for romance magazines] at night" to support her three children as a single mother, Taylor "was ready to do something else. So I wrote a book called *Love Image* [now out of print], which wasn't terribly serious. It's kind of a readable book, about a fifteen-year-old child star in Hollywood being groomed for adult stardom who discovers that she's gay, and, in order to join her first lover, has to run away."

Love Image was followed by *Prism* in 1981, then *Ripening* in 1988, and *Rice and Beans* in 1989. In discussing her reborn career, Taylor offers an unusual explanation for her literary inspiration. "I have had books, I think, given to me by the Goddess," she explains. "I'm not superstitious, but I can't account for it any other way."

Of the idea for *Prism*, a story of late-life lesbian love, Taylor relates, "I was going to bed at a friend's house in the Catskills [in upstate New York], and while I was getting ready for bed, this whole book came into my head: characters, plot, people's names, setting, everything. All the details. And I thought, ah, well, you know, it's like dreaming a book; when you wake up in the morning, it's gone. So I went to bed thinking little of it, and when I woke up in the morning, I still had it. So I wrote it."

Of *Rice and Beans,* a story of working-class life

in Tucson, Arizona, where Taylor now lives, she says, "[A few] years ago, I went to apply for food stamps—having a reputation as a writer doesn't necessarily mean you have any money in your pocket—and the food stamp situation was excessively [desperate]. I suppose it is everywhere, but in the Southwest, where many food stamp recipients and applicants are minority-race people, they are treated with very little respect. And it's very difficult to get any kind of government aid.

"Anyway, I didn't get the food stamps, and I was pretty concerned about it. And the next morning, again, when I woke up, on a hot hot summer day, I had been given another book, which turned out to be *Rice and Beans*. That book, I feel, also was given to me *completely*, you know, with all its finger- and toenails."

In addition to such inspiration, Taylor draws on her own life to provide background for her stories. In *Prism*, "the town of Abigail is partially Margaretville, New York, where I was living," Taylor explains. "I kept trying to rearrange the town; I kept trying to put the cemetery, for example, at the other end of town, and it kept hopping back to where it was. [But] the people are totally imaginary. Well, some of the minor characters are not—the people she meets at the senior center, for example. But the woman who's the love interest, Eldora, is completely imaginary. The same in *Rice and Beans*," Taylor continues. "The people in the food stamps place are exact descriptions of the people who were there when I was there."

And in *Return to Lesbos*, Erika and Vince belong to a discussion group of gay men and lesbians that is modeled after the early homophile group, the Mattachine Society. "I was one of the organizers of Mattachine Midwest," Taylor recalls. "I was the only woman on the board for a long time. Daughters of Bilitis was the [lesbian organization], but they had very small groups. We had a DOB group in Chicago and it averaged about five people. But Mattachine was both men and women."

Although Taylor draws on real-life experience to create her stories, she points out that "all my important people are imaginary," and adds, "I like my characters. The people I write about are not great heroes, or heroines, of any kind. They're quite ordinary people. But they do try to do their best, most of them. I always feel that my main characters are people that maybe you'd really like to know. I feel very empathetic, for example, to Marty and Thea of *Rice and Beans*. They're not drawn from anybody I actually know. But I think they're good people. They do dumb things, but they're good people. And the same in *Prism*. I can empathize with Ann—I am not Ann, at all—but I can certainly empathize with Ann all the way through, and Eldora, too."

Another part of Taylor's life that appears in her stories is her love of books, particularly those by and about lesbians. "I'm a reading person," Taylor declares, adding, "There are always books in my books." For example, in *Rice and Beans*, Thea says that she knows about lesbianism from a book she's read, *Beebo Brinker* (a novel by Ann Bannon). In *Ripening*, in a scene set in 1980, Taylor describes the books by lesbian authors on Erika's bookshelves. And in *Return to Lesbos*, Frances first becomes acquainted with Erika when she buys Kate's collection of lesbian books, which Erika has donated to her friend Vince's used bookstore. As a whimsical in-joke, Taylor includes herself as one of the authors whose books Frances purchases and reads. "Yes, well, my books get a little inbred sometimes," Taylor admits with a laugh.

Taylor goes on to explain the roots of her characters' love of books. "I like literate people," she states. "My parents [were readers]. Small-town people were often very civilized, quite middle-class people. You know, you read some [books] that give the impression that an American farmer around the turn of the century was a peasant! They were never peasants! They were very self-respecting people. I think people should know their ancestors were not ignorant people.

"We don't know very much about what's happened [in earlier times]," Taylor continues. "Kids don't get stories from their grandparents anymore. We had word-of-mouth connection. My grandmother— I could tell you everything that was in my grandmother's trousseau when she married my grandfather. She sent to Boston, if you please, for fine white flannel to make her wedding petticoat."

This acknowledgment and honoring of the past is a perspective that is important to Taylor. "The young [lesbians] take [today's relative freedom] for granted," she remarks. "You can go to a bar now, and you're safe; you're not going to be busted— probably. And you have some foundation for keeping a job, even if you're out. In the old days, the *Chicago Tribune* used to print, on the front page, the names, addresses, and places of employment of everybody who was in a bar raid. Just in case your boss happened to miss it, you know, the name of his company would pop up at him.

"I think [today] we take it for granted that we can go to the local bar and visit with friends. But in the old days, you were sort of taking your life in your hands. And I think the young ones [today] take [their freedom] for granted. You fire somebody for being a lesbian, and chances are she'll haul you off to court. She may not win the case, but she's going to try."

But it is not only "the young ones" who express their convictions with such feisty dignity. Born in 1913, Taylor has a long history of speaking out for her beliefs. She recalls a time in the early 1950s when the women's magazine *Ladies' Home Journal* "used to have a very good department called 'How America Lives.' Every month they would go and visit a family—one would be a black sharecropper's family, one would be a married student and his wife living in student housing, or there would be a successful businessman and his family—so [there were] all different kinds of representative families. And I wrote [to the magazine] and said, 'Why do you not do a lesbian household?' And they were very upset, and said 'We don't think our readers would [approve].' So I wrote again and said, 'One American woman in every ten is lesbian, and I'm sure some of them read *Ladies' Home Journal.*' "

Today, Taylor is an eloquent representative for older women. "It's a terrible youth culture!" she exclaims. "I don't think that older women have had, by and large, a fair reputation in current lesbian literature." But as a still-active novelist, Valerie Taylor helps to improve the image of women of all ages with her sympathetic portraits of lesbian life, based on one simple criterion: "I like to write about the kind of people I like to know."

***

Works by Valerie Taylor: *Journey to Fulfillment* (1964; reprinted 1982, The Naiad Press); *A World Without Men* (1963; reprinted 1982, The Naiad Press); *Return to Lesbos* (1963; reprinted 1982, The Naiad Press); *Prism* (1981, The Naiad Press); *Ripening* (1988, Banned Books); *Rice and Beans* (1989, The Naiad Press)

6.

Lee Lynch

Lesbian Storyteller

Victoria, Annie, Sally, Jefferson, Dusty, Elly, Andy, Peg, Paris, Mercedes, and, of course, Frenchy; these are just a handful of the proud, feisty dykes who populate Lee Lynch's seven novels and three collections of short stories. And to many of Lynch's readers, these fictional lesbians are as real as any whom one might meet at a bar or on a softball field.

Lynch's compassionate and honest portraits of lesbian life are written quite purposefully. She started writing as a fourteen-year-old junior high

Interview conducted March 1, 1991.

school student. "The teachers got very excited and told me I was talented and gifted," she recalls. "But I came out at [age] fifteen, a year later, and I was very much strangled. I couldn't write about my real life—this was 1960. Obviously, at high school and junior high school age, you can't write about who you're feeling those [romantic] feelings for if you're a lesbian.

"So as I got older, I became more and more certain that what I wanted to do was talk about myself, my life, and make my experience available to other lesbians who were feeling strangled, as I did. I had a great desire to make it better, and I didn't have any outlet for that until I was twenty-one and therefore legally old enough to subscribe to the *Ladder,* which I did, and then I started contributing to the *Ladder.* But the *Ladder* only lasted a couple of years after that, and I suddenly had no audience at all left. So it became even more imperative to me to find a place where my voice could be heard."

At this time, from the late 1960s through the 1970s, a new era of lesbian literature began. Books that portrayed lesbian life in a positive manner began to be published by lesbian-owned presses. These developments were encouraging to women like Lynch whose only previous experience with lesbian literature was the "pulps," those melodramatic paperback novels published in the 1950s and early 1960s, most of which required that their lesbian protagonists either die tragically or be "saved" by heterosexuality.

"The pulps were my initial message that there needed to be a lesbian literature, that I needed to read about myself," Lynch recalls, "because it was such a thrill to read Ann Bannon, Valerie Taylor, Ann Aldrich. But on the other hand, I got a lot of my self-hatred and internalized homophobia from [these books]. So I hope that I'm writing partially in reaction to the mentality of the unhappy ending and the suicidal lesbian, the rotten seamy side of life. I wanted positive role models and happy endings. The heck with people who say, 'Oh, she always writes happy endings!'" Lynch laughs. "We need them. "I want my writing to reflect the life *I* lead: just plain old ordinary American life."

Lynch first realized that such writing was possible in lesbian novels when Barbara Grier, co-founder of Naiad Press and final editor of the *Ladder*, "gave me Jane Rule's *Desert of the Heart*, and then I found Isabel Miller's *A Place for Us* [later republished as *Patience and Sarah*]. I was very much inspired by those two writers to think that I could do it, too. I wanted to give other readers the experience that [Rule and Miller] had given me, the validation. Here were characters like me, that I could laugh and cry about and identify with."

Although the *Ladder* no longer existed, "with the beginning of the women's movement, there were little periodicals that came out, and I would do a little bit of writing for them," Lynch recalls. "I had been sending some short stories to Barbara Grier all along, just because I needed to share them with someone, and she suggested that I send 'The LoPresto Traveling Magic Show' to [the lesbian journal] *Sinister Wisdom*. Catherine [Nicholson] and Harriet [Desmoines] were the editors then, and they loved it! And it was really encouraging!"

63

Lynch began publishing her work in book form when "Barbara [Grier] said, 'If you write a novel, I will publish your short stories,'" Lynch relates. "She felt—and she was right—that the short stories wouldn't sell without a novel first. I had written a forty-page short story called 'Toothpick House' for *Sinister Wisdom,* and [then-editor] Adrienne Rich wrote to me and said, 'It's too long for us, but you may have the germ of a novel.' So, I strapped myself in and worked a novel out. And Barbara published that and, indeed, then she published *Old Dyke Tales.*

Toothpick House, Lynch's first novel, describes the clash of cultures when "old gays" (working-class bar dykes) meet "libbers" (college-educated feminists) in New Haven, Connecticut. The conflict is one that Lynch knew well from personal experience. "The women [of the women's liberation movement] didn't want to hear about my life, about a butchy lesbian who had come out in the bars," Lynch explains. "I didn't want to talk politics and go to meetings; I wanted to go to the bar and meet some of the girls!

"Here's the women's movement and here's this dyke from Flushing [Queens, New York City]," Lynch says, recalling her life twenty years ago. "I can remember in junior high school, this guy coming up behind me and pinching me, and I turned around and smacked him. I was a dyke! You know? And the guys in the schoolyard called me 'Butch' before I knew what it meant. So, being of the lesbian sort of mind made me a feminist before I knew the word. And then I come to the women's liberation movement, and they don't want me!" Lynch exclaims. "They don't want where I come from. They want a 'struggle within the revolution' and Marxist political stuff; they don't want a woman who opens the door for another woman, or thinks it's a turn-on to light another woman's cigarette."

Lynch recognizes that the conflict "was a class thing. Although I was going to college and [was] from a newly middle-class family, my lesbian roots were with working-class women in bars. "

Lynch's coming out among bar dykes is reflected in her loving portraits of characters like these women, including Frenchy, the hero of Lynch's second novel, *The Swashbuckler*. Whereas Annie of *Toothpick House* has her "old dyke" ways challenged by the upper-class feminist Victoria, the butch Frenchy must confront changing sexual mores when she falls in love with another butch, Mercedes, and when her gay mecca of Greenwich Village becomes home to the new generation of young and uninhibited flower children.

Lynch's sympathetic and realistic writing about the pre-Stonewall gay world has led some readers to assume that she experienced those years firsthand. She points out, "I don't have a whole lot in me from that time. I got down to the Village when I could, but I was in high school! I lived at home. And then I went off to college in another state. But I think that *The Swashbuckler* and other books like that are useful because they filter that period for people just coming to it. It's real hard to read a ['pulp' of that period] cold turkey!"

But despite the pulps' frequently despairing message, Lynch feels that today's writers should "acknowledge that we have [had lesbian] writers before, and that they've given us something. They deserve some recognition, [not] that we turn our backs on them and say, 'Well, [they] just wrote depressing books.' [They] did, but [their books] also served a major function in our lives."

For this reason, Lynch tries to reach back to what she calls "lesbian tradition" in her books. "The place names in *Dusty's Queen of Hearts Diner* came from *The Well of Loneliness,*" she notes. "[And] I've got a character [in *The Swashbuckler*] named Beebo [after Ann Bannon's character]."

And, as did Bannon, Valerie Taylor, and other literary predecessors, Lynch has created a family of lesbian characters who recur throughout several novels and short stories. *The Swashbuckler*'s Frenchy continues her story in *Home in Your Hands* and makes an appearance in *That Old Studebaker,* in addition to giving advice to Lynch in *The Amazon Trail.* Peg from *Toothpick House* is a protagonist in *Morton River Valley,* which takes place in the same setting as *Dusty's Queen of Hearts Diner.* Annie from *Toothpick House* falls in love with Marie-Christine, drinks with Sally, and plays softball with Jefferson in *Home in Your Hands,* and is featured in Lynch's novel-in-progress *Annie Heaphy* (the third book in the Morton River Valley series). And Sally tends bar at Cafe Femmes throughout Lynch's first three short-story collections.

"I get so involved with the characters that they don't go away," Lynch remarks. She points out that both *The Swashbuckler* and *That Old Studebaker* started as short stories but grew into novels because their heroes, Frenchy and Andy, wouldn't "go away."

And this is fine with Lynch's readers. "I get a lot of positive response to [placing characters in more than one story]," Lynch notes, paraphrasing a typical reaction: " 'Oh, and I saw this one here and I saw that one there, and I love that you do that!' And it's so natural to me, I don't know how *not* to do it, just because [the characters] are still alive."

Lynch says, "My dream is to not have to work a straight job, and to just [work] with lesbian literature, whether it be writing, reading—that that be my working life." But she is the first to admit that being a lesbian writer is not the best way to support oneself. "We used to say that lesbians would rather buy beers than buy a book," she recalls, "but that's no longer necessarily true. But [while] books are a priority for a lot of lesbians, some lesbians don't read. So I'm going after a market within a market."

In pursuing that market, Lynch has learned to accept one inevitable part of most writers' lives: readings. "I would get physically ill, every time," she confesses. "But you can get used to anything! And now sometimes I get sleepy, reading my own [work] over and over!"

Being in recovery also has helped Lynch to feel more comfortable reading in public. "There was a time when I did tranquilizers a lot, and liquor, and I'm just a lot healthier [now], physically and emotionally," Lynch points out. "So it's [no longer] them-against-me; we're all part of the same living organism, the lesbian living organism," she laughs.

"What I get from [reading my work] is validation as a writer, because I'm a very solitary person. I don't do well in a social situation unless I have a real specific function, like 'I am the writer' or 'I am the ticket-taker' or something like that. So when I go to be a writer somewhere, and women actually show up to hear me read, that's really a wonderful ego boost."

Lynch wishes that she had more opportunities to "go to be a writer somewhere." She admits, "I love to travel, but it's very exhausting and very expensive, and I just can't do it a lot. But when I go to a new place, what I do is I walk it, I take buses around it, I try to learn little quirks about it and learn where the lesbians hang out and where the bookstores are, the kind of cultural background of it, and then I usually end up writing a story."

Lynch's adventures in new cities also frequently form the basis for her syndicated column, "The Amazon Trail," which is published in feminist newspapers all over the country and in Canada, and collected in the book of the same name. Lynch started writing the column because, she admits, "I wanted to make some money!"

Asked what it's like for a fiction writer to share her personal life in a newspaper column, Lynch asserts, "It's the same. I have to say this: Sometimes I'm not totally accurate in my journalism, so I'm a columnist, not a reporter. That's what my column's about—reflections. I don't find [writing the column] that much different [from writing stories], because it's either going to be me or a character saying it."

Of her prolific output of books and essays, Lynch explains, "When I first started writing [as an adult, in the 1970s], I felt like I had a lot of work to catch up on, because I had stopped [writing] for [a] period of time. And all of a sudden I was thirty-three or something years old, and I wasn't going to live forever, and I had too much to say! When I realized I had *something* to say, I had so much to say.

"I wanted to make a difference," Lynch says. "I wanted to get enough words out there, enough books out there, enough stories out there, that I would touch enough lives that many lesbians would [empower] themselves. I wanted to empower people, particularly lesbians, and especially the ones who wanted to write, so that they would write. They would feel like they've had permission to write about their lives, so that our generation that came out of the women's and gay liberation era would not be the end of the line, but would go on and on and on."

Asked where she sees her place as a lesbian writer, Lynch replies, "As a popular writer, a lesbian storyteller. If we had supermarket shelves that sold lesbian books, it would be fine for me to be there. Those reach the most people."

The women whom Lee Lynch has reached with her stories have benefited from her desire to share her life as a lesbian. Lynch mentions her "fear [that], reading the lesbian literature that's coming out now, we're [writing] negative images, we're not giving ourselves hope and not empowering ourselves with our writing. I can't read a lot of that [negative material]."

The women around the bar at Cafe Femmes would raise a glass to that sentiment.

Works by Lee Lynch: *Toothpick House* (The Naiad Press, 1983); *The Swashbuckler* (The Naiad Press, 1985); *Dusty's Queen of Hearts Diner* (The Naiad

Press, 1987); *Sue Slate, Private Eye* (The Naiad
Press, 1989); *That Old Studebaker* (The Naiad
Press, 1991); *Morton River Valley* (The Naiad
Press, 1992); *Annie Heaphy* (forthcoming from The
Naiad Press, 1994); *Old Dyke Tales* (The Naiad
Press, 1984); *Home in Your Hands* (The Naiad
Press, 1986); *Cactus Love* (forthcoming from The
Naiad Press, 1993); *The Amazon Trail* (The Naiad
Press, 1988)

Everybody's Favorite Authors: From Laura, Beth, and Beebo to Lane, Diana, and Kate

Ann Bannon

Katherine V. Forrest

7.

Ann Bannon

A 1950s Icon Rediscovered

One of the most popular panels at the 1990 OutWrite National Lesbian and Gay Writers Conference was "Lesbian and Gay Writing Before Stonewall." Included among the pioneering writers who participated in that panel was Ann Bannon, who in the late 1950s and early 1960s wrote a bestselling series of "pulp" paperback novels about lesbian life. Five of these books were reprinted by

---

Interview conducted August 3, 1991. The introduction to this chapter was published previously in different form as "The Lifelines Still Hold," *Visibilities*, January/February 1991.

Naiad Press in the early 1980s, introducing a new generation of lesbian readers to Bannon's beloved characters: Beebo Brinker, Laura Landon, and Beth Cullison Ayers.

The popularity of Bannon's books over three decades was reflected in the reception accorded her at the OutWrite panel. While audience members crowded around the dais to meet all the panelists after the presentation, it was Bannon's fans who remained in adoring crowds long after everyone else had left the hall. And the gracious Ann Bannon remained as well, modestly accepting thanks from women of all ages as they told her what her books had meant to them in 1959, 1969, or 1989.

"I got this *wonderful* wave of warm good feelings from the people who read the books," Bannon recalls of the days when she first wrote what would become lesbian classics. "Many of them were themselves sophisticated and informed, but I would say the majority of them were not. They were women who felt extraordinarily isolated, who didn't know anybody else. *I* didn't really know anybody else, except when I visited New York, and I could go down to the Village. But I couldn't keep those people in my life!"

For Bannon was a young housewife living in Philadelphia when she started writing these books. "When I graduated from college, I was married. It was the 1950s, so I was doing a Donna Reed," she laughs. "I was at home, and I needed to occupy myself, and I felt as if I were full of stories; I just didn't know where to *find* them.

"And when you're very young, all you really know

is what just happened to you the year before. So I started writing a college novel, and in it was a very intense friendship between two college roommates. That was a thread that ran through the original novel, which was enormous; I think I had six or seven hundred typewritten pages, and it was a very ponderous book. But I felt very pleased to have achieved that. I mean, just to sit down and put together a book—no matter how bad it is!—is to have done something kind of unusual!

"In the meantime, I had begun to discover the early blooming of lesbian novels on the paperback kiosks at the drugstores and the train stations. I had read a couple, and they moved me. I didn't know anybody was writing about that. I didn't really know anything about the topic; you couldn't go to the library and look it up!"

Among the books that Bannon read was one by Vin Packer called *Spring Fire*. "It touched me, and I wrote to her," Bannon remembers. "By the time I had gotten [my book] into shape as a novel, I had a correspondence going with Vin. And I more or less said to her, 'Now what do I do?' And she more or less said to me, 'Now, you bring it to New York, and I will introduce you to my publisher.'

"So, off I went. My husband knew I was writing, but he didn't really know *what*. But I said that I had an opportunity to talk to a publisher. I arranged to spend about a week [in New York], and I took this enormous book, and Vin Packer kindly took me in to meet her publisher," who was Dick Carroll of Gold Medal Books.

"I handed in the manuscript, which of course

weighed, I don't know, eight or ten pounds; it was heavy!" Bannon remembers with a laugh. "[Dick] said 'You know, *nobody* is going to put this into a paperback!' This was without even having read it. I must have looked stricken [because] he said, 'Well, don't worry about it; I trust Vin Packer's judgment.'

"So Dick Carroll sat down and read the book. I went back in to talk to him, and he said, 'This is a very bad book.' I said, 'Oh, I guess you don't want it.' And he said, 'No, I'm going to tell you what to do. And if you can *do* it, we'll publish it.' So then I came back to life!" Bannon laughs.

"Dick said, 'Take this book home, and throw most of it out. [But] save the friendship between the two young women, because I think that's your story.'" That story, of course, became Bannon's first book, *Odd Girl Out,* about the college romance of Laura and Beth. But her publisher's advice startled the circumspect young author.

"When Dick said, 'Your story is really the two young women,' I was greatly taken aback, because I thought I was being very subtle; I didn't think that showed!" Bannon remembers. "I was a very proper girl from a very traditional family. And I thought of myself as very married, which was what I was supposed to do. I was constructing my life along the lines that I had been told were appropriate for a young woman in my day and age. [But] I had always had the feeling that I was different. I also had the feeling that I could easily mask that, and I would prefer to do [so], because it was much *more* interesting to be a spy in other people's worlds, than to be—how shall I say?—I wasn't quite sure *who* I was; I just knew I wasn't like other people.

"And, so, the long and short of it was that I really was taken aback that I had, in effect—in this long, rambling book—tipped my cards. But I swallowed my pride, and I went back [home], and I sat down at the typewriter, and I threw everything else out, and I concentrated on Beth and Laura. And I took [the book] back, and they said, 'We like this book, and we will publish it.'

"Somehow, Dick Carroll had recognized something that I didn't know until years later was important. And that was that these two women did not have to self-destruct; they didn't have to destroy one another emotionally; nobody had to step in and murder them, or disfigure them, or shame them, or dismantle their lives, in order for me to say, somewhere in the book, that they were happy when they loved each other.

"And I didn't know I was supposed to 'bump them off,' or undercut their happiness, or ruin their lives," Bannon notes with a laugh. "So I *didn't* do that. I just said, 'This is difficult, and it can be scary.' So Beth and Laura broke up at the end, but it was hard for them to let go. And Laura went off to find a life, feeling that she was just opening a new chapter, and that Beth had given her something. Not that Beth had taken anything away from her or that she had been diminished by this [relationship]. But most of what had been published about lesbians in the past had a tragic ending, or despair in it somewhere. So [my book] was unusual, I now realize, and it was unusual that a publisher was willing to publish it."

Odd Girl Out was not intended to be the first book of a series. "I did write a second book [unrelated to *Odd Girl Out*] that nobody wanted,"

Bannon admits. "Dick Carroll said, 'This isn't working.' So I set it aside, and I thought, I'm going to go back and follow Laura to New York; I didn't *finish* that story! So I started writing about Laura going to New York to try and get her life together, and somewhere in the first fourth of the book, Beebo walked into the story, and walked up to Laura, and that book just took off! There was a tremendous amount of energy there; I was hooked.

"I think I had kind of a love affair with Beebo," Bannon recalls, "and that brought that book to life; that gave me some momentum. And by then, I was starting to get feedback from readers, and wonderful letters from everywhere, which said, 'Do some more of this.' So, that encouraged me to continue with some additional stories, and they came and they came, and it just built itself; there was always more to tell."

In the telling of these stories, the circumstances of Laura's family background changed from the first book, *Odd Girl Out,* to the second, *I Am a Woman,* in order to set up a conflict between Laura and her father that eventually is critical to the series. When asked about the discrepancy, Bannon admits, "I didn't re-read *Odd Girl Out!* Part of the problem was that I was almost two people," she explains. "I was writing these books almost in a vacuum. These books never got public recognition. The world never took them seriously, and I was almost afraid to take them seriously. [To do so] would have meant to go back and re-read them and honor them for my own investment of thought and care and emotion and all the sensuality—to respect that in myself. And I wasn't prepared. I wasn't able to think of them in that way.

"I was wholly and passionately into [the stories] while I was writing them. But I would literally get babysitters to take my children out of the house while I wrote them. I would wait until my husband was going to be gone for a month on a business trip. I had to be alone with those characters. It was the only outlet I had.

"The whole world was telling me, 'Be a nice young conventional wife and mother, and then we'll leave you alone, and you can write your books, as long as nobody knows that you're doing it.' So I think it was a flaw in *me*, I think it was the temper of the times, but I think what happened was I failed to *honor* that part of myself that wrote.

"It was like living in your head, and never living with your real heart with a real person. So the books were *enormously* important in that way: they were an acknowledgment of who I really was." For Bannon, the result of "living your life in a room with no windows emotionally" was that her books became "very intense."

"It's really hard to exaggerate the power of the emotions that have to be checked," Bannon points out. "When a door opens, even if it's a door into the pages of a book, it's as if all that intensity flows into one place. I didn't have anyplace else to put it! I didn't *have* sustained friendships. I didn't have the relief of candor. I had to take what little I had been able to see and connect with and live as passionately as I could in it, and that became the engine that drove the books."

If Bannon regrets any part of the world that she portrayed in her books, it is the episode in *Women in the Shadows,* often lamented by readers as well, where Beebo claims to have been beaten up by a group of "toughs," while in reality she has injured herself, and killed her own dog, to try evoking sympathy to regain Laura's love. "I *know* what happened there," Bannon explains. Beebo had taken on all my own strength and energy and anger. I knew that maybe I couldn't take it—I couldn't stand some of what was happening to me—but Beebo could take it. Beebo really, in a way, had my nervous breakdown for me. And it came out in this explosion of fury. Quite frankly, it was a time in my life when I didn't know how I was going to keep going. I was—uncharacteristically for me—very down.

"I would like now to be able to go back and say, after all, it wasn't Beebo; it *was* those boys that did it. But I wrote it. And I think I was just overwhelmed with grief and anger that I was not able to express. Nobody ever knew that. I think I always presented a calm and pleasant front to the world. I never had known how to express anger anyway. So Beebo did it for me. I kept thinking, I can *be* what I seem to be, and I will *do* this; my mother did it, my grandmother did it, and this is how you have to live your life. So, you know, on the pages of this book, all of it will come out, somehow."

At the time Bannon wrote the fifth and, as it turned out, final book in the series, *Beebo Brinker,* "We had been moving a great deal," Bannon recalls of her family. "I had had two children, and, within a year or two of [writing *Beebo Brinker*], I went back to school. I continued to write, but all the writing that I did from then on was academic writing. And the day of the paperback novel was fading. I felt that part of my life was over. So, I stopped writing for a while."

And, as Bannon remembers with a laugh, "I thought that was it! I didn't expect that, in the middle of my life, [the books] would rise again!" But rise they did, republished in the mid-1970s by, "of all people, the *New York Times*," Bannon relates. "The *Times* published library editions of a couple of dozen gay and lesbian classics—that was their word for it."

After the *Times'* publishing arm, Arno Press, reissued Bannon's books, Barbara Grier of Naiad Press obtained Bannon's permission to publish the books yet again in the 1980s as part of Naiad's Volute Books series of lesbian classics. Suddenly, Ann Bannon was a famous author again—but this time, in more than name only.

"I had lived a life for fifty years that was very private, and all of a sudden it was lights, camera, action!" Bannon exclaims. She recalls, "That was kind of scary to be suddenly back as a very public person. That was the first time in my life that I stepped forward and said, 'Yes, I wrote these books; it is me, not somebody else.' "

By this time, Bannon was a professor of linguistics at a California university, and she remarks, "My colleagues took it very well. I have no idea what they were saying when I wasn't in the room! But when I was, they were very gracious, and it did not prevent me from getting promoted eventually; now I am a dean. There was no way they couldn't have known. I finally just bit the bullet; there's a faculty/staff bulletin that's published every week, and they put in what people have been doing, so I would say that I had been to such-and-such a festival, or I had spoken to such-and-such a group; and nobody passed out!" Bannon remembers with a laugh, adding, "Over in the [physical education] department, I could see people peeking out of foxholes!"

Although Bannon was busy with academic writing during the years between the publications of her books, "I stopped the creative writing. And that was hard, and it was sad, and I always felt that a big part of my life was missing. You know, if you're a writer, then that's what you are, and that's what you do, and that's how you validate your life.

"So I was terribly busy; I was doing things I valued; I was finding the courage, and the financial base, that allowed me to end a long, difficult marriage; I was raising my kids. But, again, I wasn't honoring my own gift. But I couldn't be where I am now—which is much happier, *much* happier, than I used to be—if I hadn't found a way to earn a living, if I hadn't gotten the training, the doctorate—all the things I had to do. And it just took a chunk of my life to do it.

"So, you can't help thinking about the path not taken, but here we are. And I think, by the middle of [the 1990s], I expect to be able to retire. And I expect to fill up my retirement with writing. So I won't really retire, but I will *finally* be a free woman!" Bannon laughs. "I will have the where-withal to take care of myself and to write. And that's what I would love to do."

And it is what Ann Bannon's many, many fans, old and new, would love for her to do.

Works by Ann Bannon: *Odd Girl Out* (1957; The Naiad Press, 1983); *I Am a Woman* (1959; The Naiad Press, 1983); *Woman in the Shadows* (1959; The Naiad Press, 1983); *Journey to a Woman* (1960; The Naiad Press, 1983); *Beebo Brinker* (1962; The Naiad Press, 1983)

8.

Katherine V. Forrest

Writing for a Community

When I came out in the mid-1980s, I happily
wrote to my lesbian friends in my hometown to give
them the good news. One of my friends, in her
congratulatory response letter, added a P.S.: "You
must read *Curious Wine!*"

I followed her advice, and soon became hooked on
the book's author: Katherine V. Forrest. And I
wasn't the only one. This California-based author,
who has won two Lambda Literary Awards for her
popular Kate Delafield mysteries, not only sells

Interview conducted July 14, 1990.

books—lots of books—but also inspires the kind of devotion that caused one fan, a woman on crutches, to struggle up a flight of very steep stairs to attend a book-signing by her favorite author.

"It isn't anything that I've ever adjusted to," Forrest admits, "because it isn't really anything that you're aware of. You're just a person writing books, until you actually get out to a bookstore and tour and actually speak to people. All of a sudden they come up to you, and they tell you the enormous impact of your work on their lives, and it's mind-boggling."

While Forrest says that "like most writers, I've been doing it more or less all my life," for her "the magical event was turning forty, which is always a taking-stock time. For a lot of women I know, it seems to be a symbolic and significant age. And my lover said, 'You've always wanted to write, why don't you take six months and do it?' And, of course, I really did think I could write a book in six months. Anyway—three years later—*Curious Wine* came out.

"But it took me that long to learn the craft. *Curious Wine* is my first published novel, but it's not my first novel. I did the autobiographical, get-the-ghosts-out-of-the-closet sort of book which most writers do, and which I rewrote eight or nine times. I learned to write with that book."

What is unusual about Forrest's novels is that they encompass such a variety of literary genres: romance, mystery, and science fiction. "I think that writers write what they like to read," she explains. "Growing up, I liked to read good women writers. And women were very much concentrated in genres. We've always had good women science fiction writers, good women mystery writers—that's always been true. And so I read those people.

"I think some of my best writing is in *Daughters of a Coral Dawn* and a science fiction story titled 'O Captain, My Captain,' in *Dreams and Swords*. But I like to do contemporary novels, like *An Emergence of Green,* and I want to continue doing that.

"Mystery novels allow me to do a lot of things. My whole object with the Kate Delafield series was to portray a lesbian life in process, a woman in a high-visibility, high-pressure position who is a closeted lesbian, and to explore how she deals with that. This goal has formed the guts of those books. Kate Delafield is an enormously interesting woman to me, in the way that she's evolving over the series of the books.

"Kate has looked at issues of real relevance to the lesbian and gay community. Yet I can work in that sort of framework and entertain, because I write to entertain. I don't write to preach to anybody, and I hate novels that preach. But I do want to raise the issues that are of concern to us, and the Delafield series has been a terrific opportunity to do that.

"The first book [*Amateur City*] is about abuse of power. And the issues in *Murder at the Nightwood Bar* are child abuse, prostitution, body imagery— Kate becomes involved with a woman who has had a mastectomy—and about Kate becoming an actual part of our community. *The Beverly Malibu,* with the Senator Joseph McCarthy theme, could be [a metaphor] for our community, in that the McCarthy period, with its repression and witch hunts, has never ended for us.

"In *Murder by Tradition,* Kate investigates the homicide of a gay man who meets a man in a bar and ends up dead. It wasn't quite the book that I had intended to write, but it got its hooks into me, for a lot of reasons. The fact that the victim is a gay man, and he has been stabbed multiple times, and it's a very bloody scene, and there's the spectre of AIDS, not to mention the homophobia of law enforcement in general. Plus, Kate Delafield is still in a developmental phase about her own sexuality and her own closetedness. And this book gets into that a lot more deeply. So all of those things are there for the reader to see and add up as she chooses to."

Forrest's readers are very much in her mind as she writes because of what she sees as lesbian and gay writers' responsibility to their community. She cites Naiad Press publisher Barbara Grier's comment about lesbians and gay men using our books "for clues about how to behave in the community" and notes, "When I was growing up, we didn't have anything like that; we sort of invented our lives. But today, younger people do have the books to turn to, in terms of getting some idea of the behavior and courtship and all of the other patterns of our community.

"If life does imitate art, I think that our literature has impact out of all proportion, and I think that we as writers have to be very aware of that. I really do feel quite a sense of responsibility about what I have in my books. And I think all the gay and lesbian writers do, certainly all the ones that I know of, because we have an inordinate importance to our community. I think that's very true of Black writers, too—and of most minority cultures.

"Much of my aspiration as a writer comes out of the experience of my own life, because I know that if I had had any sort of role model growing up, what a difference that would have made! I'm hungry, just terribly hungry, still, for lesbian literature, and it's why I edit books, because there's no way that we're going to have the writers we want unless we can work with them and develop them, because very few people have the opportunity that I had to be able to take the time to learn my craft. If I hadn't had that opportunity, it probably would have taken me ten years, instead of three, to write *Curious Wine.*

"But if I can work with a writer, particularly a new writer—if I have a manuscript that I can apply [knowledge of] craft and technique to—I can shorten the whole process quite a bit. And so that's one of the reasons I think editing is so important."

Forrest had already published her first novel when a serendipitous turn of events led to her current role as an editor for Naiad Press. She was attending the National Women's Studies Association Conference in Columbus, Ohio, in June of 1983, which she describes as "a watershed event in the lives of a number of people who were there.

"At that conference I met, for the first time, Tee Corinne," Forrest recalls. "I met Lee Lynch; Joyce Bright, the author of *Sunday's Child,* was there; Barbara Grier and Donna McBride [of Naiad] were there; and Ann Bannon, of course, how could I ever forget her? One of my all-time incredible heroes. That's one of the great things about being a writer,

89

that I've been able to meet some of the people who meant so much to me."

Forrest continues, "We all stayed on the campus, in dormitories, so in the evenings there would be this entire community of writers visiting up and down the halls, and we would converge in one room or another, and some of us read our work. Lee Lynch read a short story, 'That Old Studebaker,' which ended up in her collection, *Old Dyke Tales*. I listened to this story and spotted a tiny flaw in it—it was a craft flaw, a technical flaw—and I just talked to her about the story. And Barbara Grier was sitting there listening to all this with sort of big elephant ears, and the upshot of it was, I came back to Los Angeles with the manuscript of Lee Lynch's novel *The Swashbuckler* under my arm. That was the first novel I edited for Naiad."

The first book that Forrest *wrote* for Naiad was, of course, the romantic and erotic classic *Curious Wine*. To Forrest, *Curious Wine* was simply "the book that I'd always wanted to read. I hadn't read anything that conveyed the passion and the beauty of our love, and how very beautiful women are together. And that was what I wanted to do in that book; it wasn't anything more complicated than that. There's a reason why we've paid the price that we've paid for our relationships. And to me, that book celebrates the rightness and the beauty of our love."

While *Curious Wine* is famous for its explicit and erotic lovemaking scenes, it also depicts powerful emotions—powerful because they are unexpected by the women who experience them. "That's what makes them work," explains Forrest. "That's really the effect of the book. I think that love scenes should be like any other scenes in a book; they should characterize the women involved. To me, love scenes are an unparalleled opportunity to accomplish things that writers can do almost no other way.

"A lot of women have asked about a sequel to that book," Forrest adds. "And there is no way that I could. The book is about falling in love and being in love and that magical circle we walk in, when you're with that person who is beautiful in all ways to you; regardless of how she may be to somebody else, to you she's absolutely beautiful in all aspects. I simply couldn't recapture any of that in a sequel.

"That book is very special to me. I don't have my photo on the book; and at that particular time [1983], it was quite important that writers be identified, the ones who could be. But I said, 'I don't want to come between the reader and this book.'

"The book operates in the reader's head, I think a lot more so than most of the work that I've done. I've been approached for film rights but I can't see it on film. I don't think that those women should acquire shape and dimension outside of the reader's imagination. And—I don't know—it's just a personal book to me, in many ways. I've never read from it. I'm sure that I've done work that other people perceive as better, but I don't think I've written a book that I love more."

While *Curious Wine* may never be adapted for the movie screen, another of Forrest's books is due to be made into a film: the second Kate Delafield book, *Murder at the Nightwood Bar*. Will the book's loyal readers who have a picture of Kate in their minds be disappointed at her movie representation, or will they say, "That's just what I thought she would look like"?

"Yes and yes," Forrest responds. "That's the power of fiction; the strongest dimension that the writer deals with is the reader's imagination. And a skillful writer doesn't give the reader everything. That's the wonderful thing about readers: they fill in the blanks beautifully, provided you don't leave too big a blank."

Speaking again about the movie, Forrest remarks, "The screenplay was initially written by Mary Robison, who is a literary writer of enormous repute. I think looking at the movie *Desert Hearts,* and talking to Jane Rule [the author of the novel *Desert of the Heart* upon which the film was based], I learned a lot about that process, and I learned a lot from Jane's attitude toward the film, which was that the film was a second cousin to the book. I think Jane understood that there are ingredients that have to be transmuted to bring the book to the screen, because it's a completely different medium.

"Mary Robison did some marvelous things and actually brought in more sexuality than what is in the book, which I was very happy to see; I thought that might be soft-pedaled, and it isn't. And when I met with the director, Tim Hunter, he made it very clear to me that he wanted to change as little of the book as possible, because that's what he was interested in filming.

"I told him, 'If you can just simply get this woman's integrity on the screen—if we could have that sort of a portrait of a lesbian for our community to look at—I'll be very grateful.' Tim is very much behind this project, and he has an excellent reputation in Hollywood. He's not your stereotypical Hollywood director; this man was a professor of literature at the University of California, and he was drawn to the novel because of the word 'Nightwood' in the title—he's an enormous admirer of Djuna Barnes. So he's an unusual man."

That a man would be so drawn to the work of Djuna Barnes and Katherine Forrest is not something that Forrest would find uncommon or suspect, given her views on the bonding in recent years of the lesbian and gay male communities. "I believe very strongly that the men and women, our two communities, belong together," she comments. "I think perhaps we needed to be apart in earlier years, but we really belong together. There's too much we can give each other. I belong to the Gay and Lesbian Writers' Circle in Los Angeles, and I've pointed out that if we're going to be in each other's lives, we need to be in each other's work. The men need to have lesbian characters and vice versa."

When asked at what age she "came out" as a lesbian, Forrest responds, "That's an almost impossible question to answer, because I've been feeling, not only about myself but about other people, that it's not a calendar date, it's a process. And it's been a continually evolving process. Ann Bannon said that with the reissuing of her books, there she was, a professor of linguistics, and all of a sudden she's unmasked as the author of these lesbian novels. She said it was like being blown out of the closet with a cannon. So I think that, willy-nilly, that happens to you with your first published book.

"I've been changing and growing with my

community; I think we all have," she muses. "I think we're gaining strength, confidence, and power from each other. Horrible things have happened, a tragedy [AIDS] that's just of inconceivable proportions. And yet we're advancing on all fronts.

"When many of us were growing up, we felt as if we were the only one. And what we've done is we've found each other, and found out what incredible people we are." And for many of us, finding Katherine Forrest, and her honest, dignified, and sensuous portraits of contemporary lesbians, was a major step forward in that discovery process.

Works by Katherine V. Forrest: *Curious Wine* (The Naiad Press, 1983); *Daughters of a Coral Dawn* (The Naiad Press, 1984); *Amateur City* (A Kate Delafield Mystery) (The Naiad Press, 1984); *An Emergence of Green* (The Naiad Press, 1986); *Murder at the Nightwood Bar* (A Kate Delafield Mystery) (The Naiad Press, 1987); *The Beverly Malibu* (A Kate Delafield Mystery) (The Naiad Press, 1989); *Murder by Tradition* (A Kate Delafield Mystery) (The Naiad Press, 1991); *Flashpoint* (The Naiad Press, 1993); *Dreams and Swords* (The Naiad Press, 1987); *The Erotic Naiad*, co-edited with Barbara Grier (The Naiad Press, 1992)

II.
BOOK AND MAGAZINE PUBLISHERS: "FREEDOM OF THE PRESS BELONGS TO SHE WHO OWNS THE PRESSES"

Lesbian Book Publishers

Barbara Grier

Barbara Smith

SDiane Bogus

9.

Barbara Grier

Climbing The Ladder *to Success:*
Naiad Press

Barbara Grier's entire adult life has been devoted to lesbian literature: from her late-teen years as an openly lesbian booklover, seeking and collecting lesbian titles during the 1950s; to a fifteen-year stint as contributor to and, later, editor of *The Ladder*, the first national lesbian periodical, published by the lesbian organization Daughters of Bilitis (DOB); to her current position as co-founder, publisher, and spokeswoman of Naiad Press, the world's largest

Interview conducted May 12, 1990.

lesbian publishing company. But those who believe in predestination might think that Grier's vocation was inevitable. After all, Grier's mother "remembered reading *The Well of Loneliness* the summer she was carrying me," Grier says proudly.

That Grier's mother not only had read a book like *The Well of Loneliness*, but also told her young daughter about it, was not an unusual occurrence in the Grier household. "We were a family that read continuously," Grier relates. "I had read from when I had been taught to read at age three. It was taken for granted that anything in the house, including my father's medical books, could be read by me, and I did read them."

But even with such an enlightened and literary background, it wasn't until March 1957 "when I saw my first copy of an issue of *The Ladder* [that] I realized what I was going to spend my life doing," Grier recalls. "I clearly do remember the day I looked at that [magazine] and said, 'Well, this is it; this is what you're going to do.' I immediately started working for them. They were asking for help in the pages of the magazine, and I began by supplying what I could supply, which was obvious: reviews."

It was "obvious" that Grier would become a reviewer of lesbian books for *The Ladder* because she already had spent years collecting such books, a task that "began as a search, and then it became a dream, and then it became an obsession. By the time I was seventeen years old and in high school," Grier remembers, "I started haunting, in a serious way, secondhand bookstores. [The owner of one bookstore] found for me a badly stained copy of the first edition of *We Too Are Drifting* by Gale Wilhelm. I still own it; it's lovely. I love its little two-dollar-and-twenty-five-cent hardcover body with its nasty coffee stain on the front. It delighted me years later to be able to bring that book back into print [in 1984].

"But it just snowballed from there," Grier continues. "I was in love with what I was doing, and I went on collecting and reading books. I realized early on that I would have to find the books myself. So I read reviews, and read reviews, and read reviews, and searched the stacks. And, of course, I read like crazy anyway; I was a constant, avid reader, a real bookworm. And then, not too many years after that, when my lover at that time went to work as a librarian in the Kansas City, Kansas, public library, I soon thereafter went to work in a nonprofessional clerical position in the catalog department of that library, and that gave me even more access to information."

The job also guided Grier to a very influential friendship. "In the course of looking through something called the *Cumulative Book Index*, I found reference to a book called *Sex Variant Women in Literature* by Jeannette Foster, which was listed as coming out in 1956 from Vantage Press [reissued by Naiad Press in 1985]," Grier recalls. "I called my local bookstore, where a woman worked who was my secret find-all-the-books-in-the-world-that-Barbara-Grier-wants person, and I told her what I was looking for. She said, 'You know, I believe I've heard that that woman works somewhere here in Kansas City, in the school system.' "

By a process of checking the local schools,

university, and the telephone directory, Grier located Jeannette Foster, "and we were fast friends for life after that. Jeannette taught me everything she knew. She was a professional librarian who had spent her whole life reading about and collecting lesbian literature, and she taught me all the [tricks] that you go through in order to find reviews. I had been dedicated before, but I became insane in a real serious way after that."

But Grier's "insanity" served her well during her years working on *The Ladder,* where she wrote the "Lesbiana" column of book reviews. "Within a year [of starting to write for *The Ladder*], I *was* the 'Lesbiana' column," Grier states. "I didn't name it, but I became it. I wrote the reviews, and I collected the books, and I made the lists, and I kept records of everything I did. At the end of each year, I created my yearly report [an overview of books with lesbian themes published during the previous year], which was what I wanted to talk about, anyway. As far as I was concerned, if you weren't reading lesbian literature, you were not part of the world."

This last statement might sound like an example of hyperbole on Grier's part, but in fact it is a succinct summary of her feelings about lesbianism and its relationship to the written word. After all, this is the same woman who says of her writing in *The Ladder,* "I felt that my duty, my function, was to find every scrap of anything relevant to lesbians and to report on it. I took that as a life function."

Indeed she did. "I became *The Ladder's* editor in 1968—primarily for the same reason I got to do everything else on *The Ladder*—nobody else wanted to!" Grier explains. "I liked what I was doing. I thought it was the be-all and end-all of the world. I thought the future of human civilization—read there, 'Lesbian Nation'—depended on the pages of that magazine. I really believed that we were going to save the world for the lesbians, and this is how we were going to do it."

Grier wielded her mighty pen in *The Ladder* much more often than the casual reader might have noticed, since she wrote under a handful of pen names, including Vern Niven, Lennox Strang, and the one by which Grier is most widely known, Gene Damon. "When I started writing for *The Ladder*, the first thing Phyllis Lyon [co-founder of DOB and *The Ladder*'s first editor] said to me was 'Well, you have to have a pseudonym,'" Grier recalls of the era when being a known "deviant" could cost a lesbian her job. "So I picked Gene Damon: Gene, because I'd always liked and wanted the name, and Damon, because it means, literally, 'the devil' or 'demon,' which I thought was quite romantic.

"And then I just added names, and they're family names. Vern Niven—I'm a fifth cousin to the late [actor] David Niven. Lennox Strang—that became, through a 'typo' in the pages of *The Ladder*, Lennox Strong. But King Strang, the Mormon king of northern Michigan, is my great-grandfather on my father's side. Marilyn Barrow—I've forgotten where I got that from; I think I picked that out of the air."

Grier's—or rather, Gene Damon's—tenure as editor of *The Ladder*, from 1968 to 1972, coincided with the beginnings of the women's liberation movement. "If you look at the history of the times, it was necessary for lesbians to walk away from the close intimate tie to the male homosexual world, and to walk more strongly toward women's liberation," Grier asserts. "And it seemed clear to me and to Rita Laporte, who was the [national] president then of DOB, that the place to go was to take the magazine away from its purely lesbian doctrinaire point [of view], and its tie to the gay male movement of the time, and to move it toward women—even though [straight] women were not only *not* welcoming us with open arms, they were running screaming up the walls, shrieking 'Lesbian! Lesbian!' at every opportunity," Grier notes. "But that was the way it was then."

The disparity of views between Grier and Laporte, on the one hand, and Daughters of Bilitis, on the other, about the direction of *The Ladder* led to a controversial resolution. As Grier admits bluntly, "In 1970, Rita and I literally divorced *The Ladder* from DOB—i.e., we stole it. We took the magazine away and turned it into a very strongly women's liberation magazine, although it stayed purely lesbian. We went into a much more political arena."

The Ladder lasted only another two years after the "divorce." "*The Ladder* failed because we ran out of money," Grier explains. "The kinds of people who would advertise in an openly lesbian magazine in 1972 were the kinds of people that, if I had put their ads in, the women would have mobbed and killed me!

"There were no lesbian publishing companies. There were no gay and lesbian bookstores. There were no lesbian services. There was no lesbian commerce. There was no cohesive world like we know today. So there was no way that I could reach out and get the kinds of advertising that magazines and newspapers take for granted now. As a result of that, *The Ladder* simply ran out of money. I thought we could keep going; we did not."

But *The Ladder*'s demise did not end Grier's "life function" of communicating with and supporting lesbians. Shortly after the last issue of *The Ladder* was published in the fall of 1972, "Anyda Marchant and Muriel Crawford, two women who were already retired, wrote to Donna [McBride, Grier's partner] and me. I'd been in correspondence with Anyda; in fact, she had done some writing in the last two issues of *The Ladder* as Sarah Aldridge. Anyda and Muriel wrote to us and said, 'We can put a little tiny bit of money up—we've always wanted to do a lesbian publishing company—will you and Donna do the work?' And that's how The Naiad Press was born.

"So Naiad, as I'm happy to tell women when I do public-speaking events, is after all just like a lot of things: a self-publishing operation. In effect, Anyda put two thousand dollars up to publish her first book, *The Latecomer,* which is still in print in 1993.

In addition to starting as a self-publishing venture for Marchant/Aldridge, Naiad was "like a lot of things" in that it began as a part-time enterprise that Grier and McBride struggled to fit in around their "real" jobs. "The first nine years, Donna and I held down our jobs and did Naiad at night and on weekends," Grier recalls. "We'd moved from the Kansas City area to Florida so that we could be nearer to Anyda and Muriel. Finally, Donna sat me down, and she said, 'We cannot go on working all night every night, and all day every weekend, on Naiad. You have to quit your job and be Naiad Press.'

"So I did that, in January 1982, which, coincidentally, corresponds to the issuing of *Faultline*, by Sheila Ortiz Taylor, which was our first spectacular bestseller. Six months later, Donna quit her job—and the bottom fell out of our business for about three months. I was scared to death," Grier remembers. "I thought we were going to go under. I don't know why the bottom fell out; those kinds of things just happen in business, and I now take those periods for granted. But that's how we began. And it was the smartest, wisest thing we ever did."

Naiad's extensive catalog of lesbian books is composed almost exclusively of fiction—novels and short-story collections. Grier says, "I share with Jeannette Foster the belief that a single work of fiction from a relevant era tells you more about what the people were really doing and thinking in that era than five hundred works of nonfiction."

And it is Naiad's reliance on genre fiction that has contributed to its financial success, since its books frequently are distributed in venues outside of the expected women's and lesbian/gay markets. "Mystery bookstores carry all of our mysteries, not because they're interested in lesbians, but because they carry mysteries, and they don't care whether there are aardvarks or antelopes or oysters in the books; all they care about is, they're mysteries," Grier points out. "The same is true for science fiction, and even for romances.

"There are about a half dozen books out that analyze romance writing for women, and often those books have a gay and lesbian section in them. And a lot of those [authors] had interviewed me when they wrote those books, because they see that [lesbian romance] is a legitimate subgenre of their field of interest. After all, some lesbians read romances, just like some straight women read romances."

While some critics belittle Naiad's preponderance of romances and mysteries, Grier notes that she is publishing for her readers and not for the "literary establishment." "People who like literature for literature's sake have a strong tendency to take seriously only those books which are somber," she declares. "I'm not talking about ordinary people who walk into a bookstore and buy books to read because they like to read. I'm talking about people who control the review media." Grier adds, "I myself find [romances] dreadfully boring, but I publish them because there are a lot of women out there who really like them. And they have a right to."

Barbara Grier's air of optimism and conviction, and her absolute dedication to all things (and women) lesbian, are the signs of a woman who has always known what she has wanted from life, and who has made sure she's gotten it—with no compromises. "My life has been a dream come true," Grier reflects. "I am absolutely convinced that the solution to our problems is to be public, be out—be really out and do exactly as we wish to do. Now, I'm not advocating running through the streets with a machete. I'm simply saying that women have a terrible tendency—more than men do, I think—to lead lives of quiet desperation, to refuse to step out and live.

"And lesbians do have clear advantages over the

rest of the world. If they would start living those advantages, they could live very positive, happy, upbeat lives. They may not live quite as insanely as I do, because not everyone wants to work fifteen hours a day. But all those [good] things are possible." And, listening to Barbara Grier, one doesn't doubt it for a minute.

A final note: On October 5, 1992, the entire collection of lesbian and gay books, manuscripts, memorabilia, periodicals, correspondence, pictures, clippings, etc. that were archived by Barbara Grier and Donna J. McBride (beginning in 1946 when Barbara was sixteen) were sent by eighteen-wheeler truck to the San Francisco Public Library. This collection of lesbian and gay literature, believed to be the largest in the world and valued at $400,000, will be used as the cornerstone collection in the Gay and Lesbian Center at the San Francisco New Main Library. This Gay and Lesbian Center will be opened in 1995 (when the library is completed), and they have pledged to preserve, protect, and make totally accessible this incredible treasure to succeeding generations of lesbians and gay men.)

Works by Barbara Grier: *The Lesbians Home Journal* (Diana Press, 1976); *The Lavender Herring* (Diana Press, 1976); *Lesbian Lives* (Diana Press, 1976); *Lesbiana* (The Naiad Press, 1976); *The Lesbian in Literature, third edition.* (The Naiad Press, 1981)

10.

Barbara Smith

Changing the World: Kitchen Table: Women of Color Press

"I'd never dreamed about being a publisher; but I always dreamed about being a writer." Barbara Smith is frustrated. As she remarks to her interviewer, "Just the fact that you're beginning the interview by asking me about Kitchen Table [Press] as opposed to [asking] 'Why did you want to be a writer?' shows the degree to which Kitchen Table has really infiltrated my life and my career and my work."

Interview conducted January 13, 1991.

And it's true that, although her powerful and sensitive essays have been widely published and anthologized, Barbara Smith's name usually, in lesbian, feminist, literary, and women of color circles, is paired with that of Kitchen Table: Women of Color Press, of which she is a co-founder and the current publisher. "The first discussions about Kitchen Table were in the fall of 1980," Smith remembers. "Audre Lorde called me and she was saying how we really needed to do something about publishing, because, as women of color writers who were feminists, we'd experienced a lot of negative things trying to get our work published, particularly in a feminist context. I was quite aware myself of how difficult it was for us, as women of color, not just to get our work published, but to have some control over what happened during that process. So [a group of us] had a meeting in Boston in November 1980, and then, a year later, we officially founded ourselves; we announced ourselves at a Women In Print conference."

In its ten-plus years of existence, Kitchen Table has published such renowned books as the anthologies *Home Girls: A Black Feminist Anthology,* which Smith edited, and the second edition of *This Bridge Called My Back: Writings by Radical Women of Color,* edited by Cherríe Moraga and Gloria Anzaldúa, and originally published by Persephone Press in 1981. More than numbers of books sold, though, to Smith, "Our major success is that we have gotten our books to as wide a range of people of color as we possibly could, and that those books have made a difference in the lives of women of color in the 'real world.' That means that there is some more understanding of the issues and realities of the lives of women of color."

While Smith's position as publisher of Kitchen Table has led some people to regard the press as one designed specifically for the works of African American women such as herself, Smith points out that "that's not a universal perception. I think that my visibility and that of, say, Audre Lorde, who was another initial co-founder, as well as a number of the works that we've published, give that perception.

"The way that it gets changed, of course, is to publish many more books by the diversity of women of color in this country. We did two major books a couple of years ago by Japanese American women [*Desert Run: Poems and Stories* by Mitsuye Yamada and *Seventeen Syllables and Other Stories* by Hisaye Yamamoto, both 1988], and I'm sure that there are Asian American people who don't know anything about Kitchen Table except that we did two important books by Japanese American women writers.

"[But] whatever the perceptions are of Kitchen Table, it has always been a press for all women of color," Smith declares. "And I think there are other ways that we have made a commitment to that, besides title by title, in who and what we publish. We have sought out manuscripts from all kinds of women of color. Not all of those projects end up as books. But the thing is that there has been support of writers from all racial, ethnic, and nationality groupings.

"Also, there has been a commitment to getting the books that we do publish to various audiences of people of color," Smith asserts. "We've always prioritized people of color events, particularly if they have a literary, artistic, or cultural perspective, or a political perspective that's appropriate to what it is we do. What we've published is not the only way that we have made good on our commitment to support the writing of all women of color."

Kitchen Table also is committed to readers, as well as to writers, of color. "I think that every organization, to be successful, has to have a focus," Smith notes. "And we chose, as our target audience, the most difficult audience to reach. Because it's not going to be any problem for us to get our books to white feminists, to lesbians, and to gay men. What will be a real challenge is to get the books and the *ideas* to people of color who may never have related to the women's movement, who may indeed be homophobic—those are the people we really want to shake up. So, of course, we're going to put more effort into that."

Still, Smith says, "I think it's important for white women to read about the experiences of people who are different from themselves. If you only read books by people who look exactly like you, and who have the same identities that you do, then you are participating in intellectual or literary segregation. I feel that books are great windows. I think that they can be a way for people to begin to see, as real, people very different from themselves, and to take us seriously and to connect with us in some very important ways, both politically and emotionally.

"[But] it's not enough merely to read. There [are] some white women I've seen who think they're experts on women of color because they've read all the right books. If they are not trying to challenge Apartheid U.S.A. in a very visceral and daily way, in tandem with other people, going into those places in their communities where other people are fighting racism as well as other oppressions—if they're not doing that, they can read all the books in the world—[that's not enough]!"

But while Smith believes that knowledge from books needs to be accompanied by work in political movements, she does not favor activism *without* some intellectual foundation. "Anybody who is serious politically better be reading something!" Smith exclaims. "There's an integral relationship between activism and ideology, and activism and theory. [Activists] at least need to read movement history, and find out about other times when people really got together to make a difference."

To Smith, "Good writers capture the consciousness of a historical era, of a movement, of a people. But they put it down in a form that allows people to respond to that lived reality in a way that no other form can. I know that the visual media has completely taken over as far as most people's way of getting information. But I think that well-thought-out prose and poetry will always have an impact in a society. Everyone needs to be literate, and we need to provide things for our children to read."

Smith is very specific about what it is she'd like to see people reading. "I'd like to see writers [with] the kind of power and politics that have characterized the work of people like Audre Lorde, Pat Parker, and perhaps myself," Smith explains, "because I think that it really is that political and radical revolutionary stance that gives the writing of those other two women, and hopefully myself, the power.

"I really am not into belles lettres, and I'm not into careerism, and I'm not into light reading. I really feel that literature, if it's going to do its work, should be about changing the world and changing consciousness on an incredibly profound level. It's not enough just to have a lot of writing available."

Not that Smith necessarily sees "a lot of writing available" by women of color. "When I go into women's bookstores, looking for writing by women of color—particularly lesbians of color—I don't see very much," Smith declares. "The situation of most lesbians of color is quite hampered by the realities of economic oppression, racism, sexism, and homophobia. That combination of oppressions really mitigates against [having] the time to be a full-time, or even a half-time, professional writer, and it also can cut into people's confidence about their capacity to do that."

Smith would like to see more "writing from lesbians of color that has great power because it is politically radical and revolutionary, as well as incredibly well crafted, interesting, original, and insightful. The kind of writers who made me want to write were people like James Baldwin and Lorraine Hansberry. Langston Hughes, too, because he was very political. That's what made their writing great—besides the fact that they were, in their own different ways, wonderful craftspeople. That's the reason that their work will last longer than that of people who are much more into the wonders of their introspective souls, or whatever." And, notes Smith,

"That's one of the reasons I think it's very important for Kitchen Table to continue to grow and flourish, because only with the institutions that support writing by women of color will we begin to see more [such writing]."

What about Smith's own writing? What would she be writing if Kitchen Table didn't take up so much of her time? "I have never stopped writing!" Smith points out. "[But] the major thing I haven't been able to do is to concentrate on writing fiction. I want to complete a collection of short stories. I guess I'm probably a slow writer as far as fiction is concerned. But I really know that I can't be bogged down with the details of running the press on a daily basis [and still write]."

"But I also, at the very same time, would not be able to just be cavalier about it and say, 'Well, whatever happens, happens—I'm cutting out of here and doing my own stuff.' Because I think there's too much of an investment in the success of the press, and the existence of the press is too important, to treat [it] in that fashion."

Returning to the subject of her own writing, Smith continues, "I plan to do a collection of my nonfiction prose, which at this point is sizable. And that's a project that I think I can do, whether I [am] 'on sabbatical' or not, because that is writing that already exists in finished form.

"Then, I would like to do a critical work on Black women's literature, since I was one of the first people in the country to really begin to teach and define that field. I'm not greatly satisfied by a lot of the work out there by Black women academics about Black women's literature, because for me it's not feminist enough, it's not political enough, and it's often homophobic."

Given the lack of published work by politically progressive African American lesbians and feminists, does Smith ever feel forced into a position of having to "represent" lesbians of color? "Well, the thing is, that's tokenism," she responds. "Anybody who belongs to even one oppressed group, and who speaks out, and is visible, is generally tokenized by people who are of small mind. But that's not who I'm writing for, and that's neither going to stop me nor keep me going.

"What really keeps me going is the wonderful response that I get from all different kinds of people who value the kind of work it is I do. I really hate to think that people are reading me and thinking this is what all Black lesbians are like! But I would hope that people would read me because I am political, and I do have a commitment to movement-building, and to representing and embodying the concerns of various women of color. A logical response [to reading my work would be], 'Oh, these are issues that affect Black women and lesbians of color, and they're being articulated by one individual, and reading what this person is saying really motivates me to want to change, and think about things differently.' That would be a more appropriate response.

"But, yes, of course, as a person who has multiply oppressed identities, I've been tokenized. But as I said, that is not a motivation," Smith adds with a laugh. However, Smith is motivated by the reactions of younger activists to her work. She says of "the young activists that I meet of all races and both genders and all sexual orientations" that "one of the things that touches me so much about them is that they seem to be inspired by the things that I've tried to do. I love the fact that, despite that generation/age gap, they see me as someone who has something to offer them, and that's beautiful!"

Smith is careful to add, "I do care about what the people who are older than me think, because I have this kind of inbred respect for my elders, which I think is very Black, you know. [And] it's not that I'm not concerned about my peers, at all! It's just that it's often one's own people in one's own age group that give one the most grief, you know, about 'Why do you have to be "out"?,' 'Why couldn't you do this?,' 'Why couldn't you do that?,' 'Why do you think this?' "

Smith laughs. "You know what I'm saying? And my feeling is, 'So what?!' If they can't hang with my reality to that degree—because I'm not asking them to live it—I'm just saying, 'Hey, this is who I am.'

"But I love the fact that, [with] people who are removed by a generation, there's a glimmer of recognition that 'Yes, we do need to dismantle this system. We do need to dismantle capitalism. We do need to eradicate, and obliterate, racism, and sexual oppression, and violence, and homophobia.' And I love that! That's great! Because if you can communicate with young people in this society, and if they communicate with you, then you are probably doing something right. Now, the people who are my age who are sitting in Congress and doing other kinds of things that really are absolutely reprehensible—do I really want them to approve of me? No, not really."

117

The approval and respect that Barbara Smith has earned from so many of us come not from Smith's trying to meet the standards of others, but from her speaking and writing from her conscience, intellect, and heart. It may be a while before her own ideals allow Smith the time to sit down and write those short stories she's been postponing for so long. Fortunately, we have her eloquent essays and speeches to sustain us while we wait.

Works by Barbara Smith: *Toward a Black Feminist Criticism* [pamphlet] (Out & Out Books, 1977; distributed by The Crossing Press); *Yours in Struggle: Three Feminist Perspectives on Anti-Semitism and Racism,* co-authored with Elly Bulkin and Minnie Bruce Pratt (Long Haul Press, 1984; republished by Firebrand Books, 1988); *All the Women Are White, All the Blacks Are Men, But Some of Us Are Brave: Black Women's Studies,* co-edited with Gloria T. Hull and Patricia Bell Scott (The Feminist Press, 1982); *Home Girls: A Black Feminist Anthology* (Kitchen Table: Women of Color Press, 1983)

11.

SDiane Bogus

Hope, Joy, Optimism, and Publishing: WIM Publications

When SDiane Bogus was a young girl, she began to write poetry, motivated by envy of her two brothers' writings in the school newspaper. Her mother's subsequent proclamation that Bogus would someday be a writer inspired her to write with great fervor.

Interview conducted December 15, 1990. The biographical information in these opening paragraphs is from the essay "To My Mother's Vision" in SDiane Bogus's book *Dyke Hands & Sutras Erotic & Lyric* (WIM Publications, 1988).

But her mother's death when Bogus was fourteen caused her to stop writing—a creative silence perpetuated by the lack of support experienced by Bogus and other Black students in their Birmingham, Alabama, high school. It wasn't until Bogus moved on to college—and to loving relationships with women—that she began to write again. A poem she sent to African American poet Nikki Giovanni was accepted for an anthology, *Night Comes Softly,* and Bogus's work was published in *Black Flame,* the newspaper of Miles College in Birmingham, where she taught after graduate school.

Encouraged to write and publish by her colleagues, Bogus began gathering the poems that would comprise her first book-length manuscript, *I'm Off to See the Goddamn Wizard Alright!* But a relationship with a female student led to Bogus's being fired by the college, and she moved to Chicago, where she taught high school and established contact with such well-known African American poets as Haki Madhubuti and Gwendolyn Brooks, to whom the overeager Bogus once delivered an unsolicited poetry manuscript—arriving, to her own chagrin, at 7:30 on a Saturday morning! However, many of these established poets found Bogus's work too political, and so she published *Wizard* herself in 1971, selling her full run of four hundred books as well as sending copies to such celebrities as Johnny Carson and Aretha Franklin. While Bogus was not asked to read her poetry on the "Tonight" show, a librarian to whom she had sent a review copy did arrange for her to be interviewed on the Black talk show "Harambee" on PBS.

In 1973, Bogus moved to California, where she

compiled her second poetry manuscript, *Woman in the Moon*. On two separate occasions, women publishers offered to print this collection; both offers fell through, and so, once again, Bogus self-published her work, eventually establishing her own press, WIM (Woman in the Moon) Publications. Bogus founded WIM in 1979; her lover T. Nelson (Trilby) Gilbert joined WIM as business manager in 1989.

Though WIM is today best known as publisher of Bogus's work, it is not a "vanity press." WIM primarily publishes poetry, encouraging writing by lesbians and other women, African Americans, and prisoners, and sponsors (in conjunction with the National Women's Studies Association) the annual Pat Parker Memorial Poetry Award for work by Black lesbian poets. WIM also publishes nonfiction books as diverse as *The Lesbian and Gay Wedding Album* and *Who's Who in Mail Order*.

"We generally are looking for work that's enlightened and enlightening, that uplifts the human spirit," explains Bogus, adding, "I'm waiting for a surprise to come across my desk. I'm really looking for the kind of people who have been able to match spirituality and sexuality together, or who have found some truth beyond race differences. And I'm not looking for the usual platitudes about 'We all can live well together' [so much] as I'm trying to look for some insights into how someone has come to a kind of peace in living well with someone else, and they speak of it from that place."

WIM has become well enough known that manuscripts are regularly submitted for consideration. Bogus has made sure that her company's name is before the reading and writing public, through

WIM's catalog, its listing in directories and trade journals, and Bogus's appearances at conferences and trade shows.

But when asked how WIM supports itself, Bogus laughs. "This is a joke!" she responds, but continues, "Primarily, maybe about 35 or 40 percent of how this press is sustained is through my salary as a teacher, and my performances. So generally, whatever goes into the press, to sustain it from month to month and day to day, is from what I put in, personally.

"Then we have about fourteen books in print, so maybe about 20 or 25 percent of the money that helps sustain the press comes from book orders, from jobbers at bookstores. Then about 15 percent of it comes from other sources—miscellaneous individual orders from people at trade shows and such. And we advertise in mail-order publications all over the country for some of our sideline products [mailing lists, tapes of poetry readings]."

Despite WIM's ambitious catalog, it is the publisher herself who is WIM's most famous "product." Bogus is so prolific, and her work covers so many genres, that even she has admitted that her audience has been scattered. "I started out as a science fiction writer and a reviewer," Bogus explains. "And I had written lots and lots of poems; I was publishing my books of poetry even while I was making my career as a [prose] writer. I've had audiences in the lesbian/feminist community, the Black community, fantasy and science fiction, as well as the general poetry market. And now, I'm publishing academically, so I've got [several] audiences for what I write.

"So that gives me a much wider appeal than I had early on. But my readers didn't know who I was all together; I didn't have the body of my work located in any central place. But in these last seventeen years, since I came to California and I've been writing here, it's all come together."

Reading the clippings in WIM's press pack, one realizes that SDiane Bogus, the "personality," is perhaps more famous than SDiane, the poet, or Dr. Bogus, the publisher. "It's quite purposeful," Bogus admits of her self-promotion. "I got the idea from Gertrude Stein. You know, Stein's personality outshone her work. She created herself as an influence and a personality in writing. And then people got more and more into her work as they got more and more interested in her. They wanted to know who this woman was. And, as yet, her legend is still being explored.

"So, I figured, all [you] have to do is create yourself as someone to explore, and then the questions of what you talked about, and what you had to say, remain on the planet after you're gone!"

What Bogus has to say is something even she can't predict. "I'm under the direct influence of the universe; whatever that turns out to be, I'm not sure," Bogus muses. "It's like at the [1990] OutWrite [Lesbian and Gay Writers'] Conference, when I was asked to speak as part of a panel during one of the plenaries. I got up to tell them a little about the history of WIM Publications, and something came over me that day that said I had to tell the people about natural order.

"And so, in some ways, I have no idea, fully, what my message is. All I know is that it's one of hope. It's one of joy. It's one of optimism. In whatever ways I can find to express that. So you won't hear me bashing people, and you don't hear me talk much about racism, or talk about sexism, in that way. There are other writers who do it so much better than I. I'm always trying to find a way to speak of sexism, racism, homophobia—whether they are painful to me or not, and whether I'm experiencing them in those ways or not—[in ways] that will uplift and enlighten. That's the work I find myself doing.

"In terms of my audience, it's real difficult for me. Depending on which audience I'm talking to, I talk with the same optimism and with the same amount of joy and enthusiasm, but it just depends on what I feel needs to be said.

"Now, in terms of Black people, for example—and this is Black straight people, because I'm assuming my *Black* community at large is heterosexual—I talk to them about matters of freedom, and matters of integrity and character. I gave a talk to a group of Black women who call themselves the Black Women's Network. And it didn't seem to matter that I was a lesbian. They know very well that I am, they just didn't talk about it, and I didn't ask them to talk about it, you see what I'm saying? I don't make demands of my audience that they're not asking for; I just perform the service as required. As a result, I end up wherever I'm supposed to, saying what I am given to those who have ears to hear.

"So, I'm trying to think now, what is the compromise, which parts of this whole thing can I embrace and still be alive, and what part of them can I talk to other women about? In *The Chant of the Women of Magdalena,* I talk about women forming a community where all their gifts and talents are brought to bear, because they are outside the range of men, but they are not without the kind of structures that informed you and me. And I try to show what the possibilities or probabilities are, given that we are all informed by patriarchy, we are all very entrenched in it, pretty much in the same way that Audre Lorde talks about how none of us could be free of the effects of racism in this country because it's so insidious."

Bogus takes her ideas, and her expression of them, very seriously. She explains, "Early in my career, I had no following; all I had was the appreciation of my mother for my poetry, and the recognition of some of my teachers for it as well, and the assurance that I had the gift to write. [At that time] it was just enough to have a limited principal audience congratulate me and be proud of the fact that I could do these things.

"But the more I wrote, and the more I grew, and the more often I had an opportunity to publish, the more I started to realize that there was some more in the offing, that I could actually start to affect people's minds. And so then I started to think, there is at least a vision of being able to write where it was meaningful to other people. So now, that's my *intention!* My family is proud of me and they love me for what I'm doing, and people do love my work—that's fine! But now I just want to know that

I'm leaving some kind of legacy that will make a difference, that's all."

Bogus realizes that her "legacy" doesn't please everyone. "Sometimes I refuse to see things in black and white," she concedes. "Because if I really get caught up in the 'isms' of this world, it would be virtually impossible to really offer anything constructive, useful, helpful, and enlightening, and so all I'd do is just be another part of the problem, not be someone who's trying to offer some solutions. It seems to me that people are going to be moved to take more and more negative action if more and more people don't continue to speak the possibilities of real loving action. There are just not many people *able* to do that. So those of us who have gotten just (spiritually) free *enough* to be able to speak, do so. It is simply our work to do.

"For some people, my work is not political enough; for some people, it's too idealistic or too visionary. But it's the stuff of which I'm made." Faith, self-confidence, ambition; indeed, this is the "stuff" of which SDiane Bogus is made. And her legacy is more than her poetry, more than WIM Publications. It's her optimism and her conviction. "We're going onward and upward at every turn," Bogus declares. "I'm not ashamed to believe with faith that things are changing for the better, that all things do work together for good, for those who hold that vision."

Works by SDiane Bogus: *I'm Off to See the Goddamn Wizard Alright!* (WIM Publications, 1971); *Woman in the Moon* (WIM Publications,

1979); *Sapphire's Sampler* (WIM Publications, 1982); *Dyke Hands & Sutras Erotic & Lyric* (WIM Publications, 1988); *The Chant of the Women of Magdalena* (WIM Publications, 1990); *For the Love of Men: Shikata Gai Nai* (WIM Publications, 1991)

A Magazine of One's Own

Lisa Ben

Carol Seajay

Franco

Toni Armstrong Jr.

Lisbet

12.

Lisa Ben

"America's Gayest Magazine":
The First U.S. Lesbian Periodical

During the years following World War II, there

Lisa Ben's statements in this chapter are quoted from her taped remarks at a gathering held on July 12, 1988, as well as from written questions and answers in an exchange of letters between Kate Brandt and Lisa Ben dated August 15, 1989, and August 28, 1989, respectively. Portions of this chapter have been published previously in different forms as "Lisa Ben: A Lesbian Pioneer" in *Visibilities*, January/February 1990; "An Evening with Lisa Ben" in the *San Francisco Bay Area Gay and Lesbian Historical Society Newsletter*, September 1988 and Winter 1988; and "Lisa Ben: A Blast From the Past" in the *San Francisco Sentinel*, July 22, 1988.

were no lesbian presses, or magazines, or bookstores. It wasn't until the late 1950s that paperback novels with lesbian themes—most of which were melodramatic and given to tragic endings, and many of which were written by men under female pseudonyms—were widely sold along with other softcover "potboilers." In 1956, the national lesbian organization Daughters of Bilitis (DOB) began publication of a journal called the *Ladder*. This periodical, which was published until 1972, is popularly regarded as the first lesbian magazine.

But if you were a literary-minded lesbian who lived in the Los Angeles area in the late 1940s, you might know otherwise, because you might have been a reader of a lesbian review called *Vice Versa*, edited by one Lisa Ben.

Vice Versa was by no means a slick, glossy journal. In fact, its own creator calls it a "little homemade magazine." But its reason for being, and its message, are as sophisticated as anything published by an activist group today. As an essay in the first issue (June 1947) titled "In Explanation" states,

> There is one kind of publication which would, I am sure, have a great appeal to a definite group. Such a publication has never appeared on the [news]stands. . . . Why? Because *Society* decrees it thus.
>
> Hence the appearance of *Vice Versa*, a magazine dedicated, in all seriousness, to those of us who will never quite be able to adapt ourselves to the iron-bound rules of Convention.

Vice Versa was created in 1947 by a Los Angeles secretary who wrote under the pseudonym of Lisa Ben (an anagram, of course, of "lesbian"). With the resourcefulness common to those who must be secretive, Ben produced *Vice Versa* at the office where she worked.

"I would type it out during working hours," she recalls. "I never had enough work; I was a very fast typist. And my boss would say, 'Well, I don't care what you do if your work is done. But I don't want you to sit there and knit or read a magazine; I want you to look busy.'

"So I said, 'Aye, aye, sir; I'll try to look busy.' So that's how I put together *Vice Versa*. I used the office stapling machine [and] manila folders, and I didn't feel a bit guilty about it! I should have, but I didn't."

Producing a publication of any sort entailed physical as well as creative labor in those days before word processing and desktop publishing. But Ben says of the process, "I had an awful lot of fun putting it together. I hand-typed it on a manual typewriter," she recalls. "I would use carbon paper, because in those days we didn't have such things as [photocopiers] or even a ditto machine. I would put in the original and then seven copies; that's all the typewriter would take legibly. I did eight copies at a time. I'd run it through twice, that made sixteen copies, and that's not very much.

"And after I was through, and put it all together, I would give it to my friends. I never sold it, I just gave it to my friends, because I felt that it was a labor from the heart, and I shouldn't get any money for it. And so I said, 'Now, when you're through with it, please pass it on to another lesbian. Don't just throw it in the wastepaper basket, because these things are not dated—they don't have anything in them of news, or anything that would be passé, just fiction and poetry and book reviews and whatnot. So pass it along.' "

Or, as an editorial in the second issue (July 1947) admonished, "Just because the magazine is gratis does not indicate that work and effort have not been expended in publishing it, so if *Vice Versa* does not appeal to you, either refuse it or pass it along to someone else. But, puh-leeeze, let's keep it 'just between us girls!' "

"Us girls," as it happened, were a side benefit of editorship for Ben. "During those days I didn't really know many girls," she admits. "But I thought, well, I'll just keep on turning out these magazines and maybe I'll meet some!

"And I did! When I turned out my first copy, I probably knew about four people. And the next month, they introduced me to some more, and I knew ten people. And so on and so on and so on. So it grew. And eventually it grew to more girls than I had copies!"

By the second issue, *Vice Versa* had added the subtitle "America's Gayest Magazine," a designation well supported by the journal's contents. Many of the articles were essays on the arts—book, film, and theater reviews—but their subjects all had lesbian themes. But just because a play or a book had some lesbian content didn't mean that *Vice Versa* championed it without reservation. In an editorial in the July 1947 issue, Ben asked, "Why not read and review one of these listed stories [in the 'Bookworm's Burrow' section] for the benefit of those who have not the time to read the book, or perhaps can not obtain it? It does not have to be a complimentary review. Don't hesitate to express your own opinions."

Finding other women to contribute material to *Vice Versa* was a constant challenge for Ben. "I asked other people to please contribute also, so I wouldn't have to do the prodigious amount of writing to fill up the magazine pages," she states.

"[But] very few people contributed. And of those who did, I was obliged to put in everything that was given to me, even though sometimes I felt that what was given me was rather silly or was material that I really didn't want to include. [But] I generally had to include it because I didn't want to hurt the person's feelings.

"So that's why every once in a while, if you have an old copy of my magazine, you'll read something and you'll say, 'My God! Did she write *that*?!' And I didn't! But most of the poetry is mine, and the book reviews."

Ben is modest about her ambitions as a writer. "I liked to read science fiction, and also fantasy and horror stories; I think I penned a couple of stories for some homemade-type fantasy magazines back in the forties," she says. "I also mailed some literary attempts to professional fantasy magazines, but promptly gave up when I received rejection slips. *Vice Versa* was my main writing activity."

Ben also writes poetry and songs, which she has been doing "since I was in grammar school. [But] if I do write something, I don't sit down and say, 'I am now going to write a song about the mountains, or a trip I took.' I can't do it that way. Something's got to move me. In my youth, I would fall in love with somebody, or somebody would make me terribly angry, and I'd write a poem to let off steam. Whether it was anger or love or happiness or whatever, it was some emotion that stirred me, and then I would write the song.

"It was almost as though it was being dictated to me. I did not feel that I had much to do with it. This [idea] would come, and I would grab a pencil and a piece of paper and I'd start writing. I don't mean automatic writing, like spiritualism, but just writing. And then I would stop for a while, and I would look over what I'd written, and then I'd make an alteration here and there, if I thought it was necessary.

"Sometimes, I'd go to bed, and a tune would come into my head during my sleep. Mostly, though, [it happened] when I was awake—I'd be on my way somewhere, doing something *utterly* different, and this tune would come to me and fit right in with the words [I had written]. It was very handy; I enjoyed this happening to me.

"But I don't know why [it happened]; I can't explain it. I guess lots of people probably have the same experience—this is probably nothing new, just for me alone. But it's fun. And to me, it was more exciting than anything I could think of, even sex. It was the most marvelous feeling that could ever happen to me."

So much so, in fact, that Ben continued song-writing and sang some of her gay parodies at "open mike" sessions in Los Angeles gay clubs during the 1950s. By that time, after producing nine monthly issues of *Vice Versa*, Ben had stopped publishing the magazine, for a very practical reason.

"The place where I worked was sold, and I had to get a new job," she recalls. "And, of course, at the new job, I had no opportunity to [produce *Vice Versa*]—it was a different setup—so I had to discontinue [the magazine]."

Ben then turned her creative talents to her songs and song parodies, substituting gay-related lyrics for those in the hit songs of the day. "I started writing parodies to popular tunes in 1948 and 1949, if I remember correctly," Ben notes. "I was absolutely appalled at the gay male entertainers who would, on stage, make derogatory remarks and dirty jokes about themselves to entertain the non-gay people who came there to be entertained and 'see how the queers lived.' No wonder society had such a bad opinion of us.

"So, I started writing parodies which would be *gay*, but not dirty or demeaning to us. I sang a few of them at one gay bar where we would all gather for afternoon dancing, before the nighttime non-gay crowd came in. I did not care to share my songs with a non-gay audience. I wrote strictly for *us*. This is my interpretation of separatism."

Ben's song parodies included such numbers as "I'm Gonna Sit Right Down and Write My Butch a Letter (And Ask Her Won't She Please Turn Femme)" and "I'm a Boy Being a Girl." Her songs were frequently inspired by events that affected her circle of friends.

"The boys used to have a kind of dive they went to which was in downtown Los Angeles, and it was called Maxwell's," Ben recalls. "It was not for the girls, so I never went down there. But it was very well known, and, unfortunately, I think they had a few raids there, too. And so I wrote this song parody called 'The Vice Squad Keeps On Breaking Up That Old Gang of Mine.'"

One of the slyest parodies that Ben wrote was a takeoff on the jingoistic Merle Haggard country-western tune, "Okie from Muskogee." "It was extolling the virtues of being square and Midwestern," Ben says of the original song. "It was very popular. And it struck me funny, and I thought, Oh, my, that needs some new lyrics! So I wrote my own words to it, and I called it 'Fairy from Tulare,'" Ben continues. "It's about two fellows that got stuck in [the rural California town of] Tulare; they're gay fellows, and they find life rather difficult there, and they want to move to San Francisco."

Ben's performing career entered another phase when she joined the Los Angeles chapter of Daughters of Bilitis. "I first heard of Daughters of Bilitis at a gathering of lesbians in a private home. I thought it was an excellent idea and joined because it gave us an alternative to just frequenting gay bars," Ben recalls.

Ben sang at the first DOB convention in 1960. One of her tunes, "The Gopher Girls," delights lesbians who hear it today, more than thirty years after it was first written and performed:

Some girls drink and some girls smoke
Some will tell a naughty joke
Some girls work and some girls play

138

And some girls lie in bed all day
Some wear skirts and some wear pants
Some go topless when they dance
Some like dogs and some like cats
But let me tell you where it's at

Chorus:
We are The Gopher Girls
We only go for girls
We never go for men
So here we go again
Have you had yours today
I had mine yesterday
That's why I walk this way
Ta ra ra boom de ay!

A "silly" song, until you remember that it was
first sung at a time and place where lesbians had to
wear three items of "feminine attire" in public to
"prove" that they were women. In that context, "The
Gopher Girls" becomes an anthem of liberation, just
as *Vice Versa,* so lovingly typed in an office where
its discovery could have cost its editor her job, is a
declaration of independence and pride. As an
editorial in the premiere issue of *Vice Versa*
declared: "If *Vice Versa* should be subjected to the
glance of unsympathetic eyes, let us at least show
that our magazine can be just as interesting and
entertaining on as high a level as the average
magazines available to the general public." Those of
us who *still* "will never quite be able to adapt
ourselves to the iron-bound rules of Convention" owe
a great debt to Lisa Ben.

13.

Carol Seajay

Spreading the Word:
Keeping Connected with
Feminist Bookstore News

Carol Seajay remembers the first women's bookstores that she ever saw, in the early 1970s. "I don't remember the physical surroundings as much as the idea and the books; books and books and books, which, in hindsight, was a tiny little collection of books," she recalls of one such place. Describing another store, Seajay says, "They had this idea that if you just put all this information about women

Interview conducted June 9, 1991.

together in one place, something incredible was going to happen. And it did."

What happened over the next twenty years was an astounding proliferation of "women's books"—lesbian and feminist writings—and the bookstores in which they were sold, including San Francisco's Old Wives' Tales, which Seajay co-founded in 1976. The writing, publishing, and distributing of these books came together in a social and political movement known as Women In Print. Its legacy includes periodicals and presses, women's bookstores (of which there now are more than one hundred in the United States), writers of all genres, and the publication that links them, *Feminist Bookstore News (FBN)*, which Carol Seajay has published and edited since 1976, and for which she received the Publisher's Service Award of the 1989 Lambda Literary Awards.

Although circulation initially was limited to women's bookstores, *FBN* now is more than a trade journal for feminist booksellers. The bimonthly publication is a treasure trove of information about bookstores, presses, current and forthcoming books, conferences, trends, and any other news relating to the lesbian/feminist publishing industry, as well as discussions and debates on issues important to that industry.

FBN is very much a product of the Women In Print movement, part of the historic era of lesbian and feminist discovery that was born of women's liberation and the Stonewall rebellion. "Fifteen, twenty years ago," Seajay explains, "there was such a clear sense that women were *not* in print. Women existed in print in the male image only—which is hard to imagine at this point in time, that there

142

really were not lesbian novels with happy endings. There was a tremendous drive to get the truth of women's lives into print. And we came to understand quite quickly that we had to control the *entire* means of print in order to guarantee that we could get into print."

For example, Seajay recalls, "There were a number of cases where women's newspapers did articles on the self-help movement—you know, a woman actually looking at her os and being able to evaluate her own vaginal health. And when these articles started coming out, there were a number of women's newspapers whose printers called photographs of a woman examining herself, using a speculum or looking up her vagina, 'pornographic' and refused to print them. At the same time, the mainstream media, when it did cover women's liberation issues, frequently distorted or trivialized them, or resorted to lesbian-bashing.

"So that made it clear to us that if we wanted to circulate this information, we had to buy the presses and print it ourselves. We had to control the typesetting; we had to do all the printing processes—the stripping, the photographing. Binderies refused to bind lesbian and feminist books, so we had to do the binding ourselves. We had to do our own distribution, we had to have our own bookstores, in order to get this [information] out into the world. And so, the Women In Print movement came to mean controlling all of the production. And it was quite heady and exciting and powerful."

Among the outward manifestations of the Women In Print movement were its national conferences, held regularly for several years. The first one, held in 1976, "was quite an event, and an extraordinary part of feminist and lesbian publishing history," Seajay recalls. She credits the late June Arnold, co-founder (with Parke Bowman) of the pioneering lesbian/feminist press Daughters, Inc., with organizing this initial event.

"June had been touring and had done a program at A Woman's Place [an early women's bookstore in Oakland, California]," Seajay recalls. "A bunch of people went off afterwards to the Bacchanal, a lesbian/feminist bar, and came up with this idea of 'Wouldn't it be great to get all the women who are working on feminist magazines and newspapers and bookstores, and the printers and the publishers, and get them all together in one place.'

"It was a great idea, but what June did was she made that idea happen. I think she put a fair amount of her own money and enthusiasm and quite a lot of time into it. And she declared a week-long conference at a Campfire Girls camp in Nebraska. Why Nebraska? Because it was the center of the country; it was an equal distance from both coasts, so no one would have to drive more from either coast. In those days, everyone drove; no one had money for plane tickets.

"About two hundred of us gathered, and it was an incredible event. The connections, both creative and personal, that were made there really influenced feminist publishing and writing and magazines for years after."

At that time, Seajay was working at A Woman's Place, and making plans to start Old Wives' Tales in San Francisco. "There were about eighteen [women's] bookstores [represented] there," Seajay says of the first Women In Print conference. "Needless to say, we had everything to say to each other. We talked and talked and talked, you know, 'Do you know a book about...' and 'What do you do when a customer does this' and 'What do you do when your community needs you to do that and you don't have the resources'—and it was just incredible! Because most of us had never talked to someone who worked in a feminist bookstore, besides our own group. It was just a very powerful way to break down that isolation and to share information.

"We were talking constantly for a week, and we didn't want to go home, and we didn't want to stop talking. Women came up with various ways to stay in touch. Phone calls were too expensive on our tiny budgets; we talked about a round-robin letter—you know, we'd start these letters and pass them on—and then some women were very realistic about the state of their desks, and that things would be caught in a stack of piles and not get passed on," Seajay laughs.

"Eventually, we decided we wanted a newsletter. And everyone thought that was great, but nobody wanted to do it." Seajay finally volunteered, because "I figured, gee, if I work ten or fifteen hours a month on this newsletter, at three dollars and fifty cents an hour, I would be much further ahead! And since I was living on about two hundred dollars a month at that point, it was a significant amount of money.

"The funding [for *FBN*] is very much a feminist concept. The five largest bookstores each put in one hundred dollars to get the newsletter off the ground. There was always an understanding that those stores

145

that could afford to, put in more, and the stores that are tiny and [staffed by] volunteers, or are just surviving, put in less. It's a sliding scale that has genuinely worked, year after year."

When asked how new bookstores became aware of and part of the *FBN* network, Seajay laughs. "Magically aware! It was on the great psychic feminist grapevine! Actually, how it worked was, as we heard of new stores we of course added them to the mailing list, and sent them *FBN*, and they would subscribe. And as other people went into bookstores and said, 'I'm thinking of opening a bookstore in —— oh, wherever, then someone would tell them, 'Well, you want to get *Feminist Bookstore News*.' Also, when new bookstores ordered books from lesbian and feminist presses, the presses would tell them about *FBN* or would inform *FBN* about the new store.

"[There's] a lot of belief in the power of sharing our resources and supporting each other. One of my main goals with *FBN* is that the magazine reflect back to the booksellers the work that they're doing. Because when you're out there, doing the work day after day, it's easy to get bogged down in the headache of it all.

"And what *FBN* does when it shows up in the mail is to say, 'Oh, but this is also a political body of work; your work is very important in a larger context.' Our communities tend to take us for granted; people will come in and tell you what you *didn't* do well enough, and forget what you did extraordinarily well!"

What is the future for feminist bookstores? Will

competition from gay male–owned bookstores added to the shaky economy of the late 1980s and early 1990s combine to make it harder for small, women-run businesses to last?

"The fact of the matter is that lesbian or feminist bookstores serve the women's community in a way that gay men's bookstores don't, and provide an atmosphere and a collection of literature that's not available elsewhere," Seajay asserts. "Long-term, I see a lot of women who've gone off to wander come home to feminist bookstores."

As for the economy, Seajay says, "Basically, we're just going to outlast economic fluctuations; I think that's the bottom line. What you have at this point, in the women's bookstore movement, is a fair amount of experience, and people being able to look at an upcoming bad economic situation and take the appropriate precautions.

"A recession is like a wave. Two years after the recession is declared to be over, it will really hit some of the areas where there are women's bookstores. But at that point, the [economy] will have recovered in the places where it's been worse. The ones that are not yet hit by the recession are carrying the load for the ones that are having a harder time. If we had a chart that showed sales patterns in women's bookstores, overall it would be consistently up.

"So it's not a panic situation at all; it's that thing that I appreciate as I get older, that there is a long term. If sexism and patriarchy had in fact been resolved over the last twenty years, then there wouldn't be a need for feminist stores. Since that hasn't exactly been totally solved, the demand for feminist bookstores is going to continue well into the future."

Seajay's vantage point as a veteran feminist also lends perspective to her discussion of those younger lesbians, many of them active in mixed-gender groups such as ACT UP and Queer Nation, who declare that women's bookstores are no longer relevant or "cutting edge." "I think it's a question of who gets media attention," Seajay explains. "I have no complaint that ACT UP and Queer Nation are getting wonderful media attention. I *like* their work; it's essential. And it's essential that each generation of young people come up and invent a world for themselves, and an activist community, and I'm delighted to see it.

"But I think there will also be an upsurge in women-focused organizing—because gay men's and mixed organizations aren't effectively addressing women's issues. Go to an ACT UP meeting and see who gets the floor space; what's the gender of the names that get mentioned in press releases? It's not lesbians. And women are getting tired of that.

"It's maddening how little media attention women get when there are women organizing around women's issues. When you have women in ACT UP, then there's more media attention, because they're working with men. Consistently, when there are women working with women, there *is* no media attention from anyone except the women's media— which is why we had to invent women's media!"

Of those women who engage in what Seajay calls "feminist-bookstore-bashing," she says, "They should speak for everything they're into, but not trash what they're *not* into." But she adds, "This is also a generational thing. The essence of coming to maturity is defining yourself. And sometimes you have to define that you're *not* something else in order to figure out what you are. If this generation coming up doesn't have any sense of history, then it's because we haven't made it available to them, and we'd better figure out fast how to put lesbian history into hot sexy novels!" Seajay laughs. "If that's the preferred mode—get it out there!"

Seajay applauds the " 'zines"—the homemade periodicals—being produced by this younger generation of lesbian activists. She remarks, "I think the 'zines are, to this generation, exactly what feminist newspapers [were] to our generation. They're very out there, and very 'Here's a vision,' and 'Here's something that has to be said,' and people slapping it down on paper, and printing it out, and circulating it, and tremendously effective and powerful and exciting. And that's very much what we were doing then, in another generational form."

Of her own creative and political writing—or rather, her lack of time in which to do such work—Seajay reflects, "I have consistently re-chosen to make *FBN* my priority. For me, it's been a pretty clear reality that unless there is a network of feminist bookstores to be selling lesbian work, there's no point in writing it, and no point in publishing it, because that's where it gets sold. And unless we have this world we created for ourselves to support lesbian writing and see it into print and sell it and promote it and circulate it, then there's not a lot of value in writing it.

"It's sometimes been a hard choice," Seajay

admits. "Sometimes I think it would have been a little easier to have been born ten years later; someone else could have figured all that out! And I could have just been a writer. Oftentimes I've thought that if *FBN* just had more staff, it would make the difference and I could go forth and write great lesbian literature."

Still, "greatness" is a relative concept. Carol Seajay may not have the time to "write great lesbian literature." But her work brings together a lesbian nation of booklovers: women who share lives and adventures and knowledge through the books that we read and write and buy and sell. And isn't that great?

14.

Franco

New Dyke in Town: *The Rapid Rise of* Deneuve

Most readers assume that the lesbian magazine
Deneuve was named for the French film star
Catherine Deneuve. But when *Newsweek* ran a short
article on the San Francisco–based periodical after
its debut in May 1991, it told the *real* story—sort of.
"They said that the magazine was named after a
woman I had a crush on!" exclaims Franco,
Deneuve's founder, publisher, and editor-in-chief, who
started the publication when she was twenty-two

Interview conducted February 8, 1992.

151

years old. "Well, that was a polite way of putting it for the straight audience. A 'crush!' "

The relationship was a little more intense than a mere infatuation, Franco explains. "It was when I was fifteen. We were co-counselors in a camp. And something just happened to me. I had already known that I liked women. But here was my bed, here was her bed, the kids would go to sleep, and we would sneak into each other's bunks. We kissed and played around, and it was a fantastic summer. I was *totally* in love with this woman.

"So after the summer ended, I called her every day—I'm surprised my parents didn't wonder why. We had planned that I would [visit her] during Christmas, [but when] I went to her house and [she] opened the door, there was her boyfriend!

"My mouth just dropped open," Franco remembers. "I didn't know what to say. I refused to talk to her. I was *so* heartbroken! And she pulled me aside and said, 'What were you expecting? What we had—that's not reality! That's not normal.' That was the last thing she ever said to me: 'That's not normal.' "

Franco returned home, decided "Okay, I'm going to be normal," and made plans to marry her boyfriend. "I told him about my feelings for women, and he thought it was a phase," she relates. Then, "One day, my husband came to me and said, 'We're going to be transferred. You have your choice: either San Antonio, Texas, or San Francisco.'

"I just looked at him," Franco recalls, "and I said, 'I hear the women in San Francisco are really cute; let's move there.' Eight months later, I was madly in love with a woman again. The marriage didn't last long after that."

But adjusting to her new lesbian life wasn't always easy for Franco. "I was very much closeted, and I was too afraid to ask anyone where to go, what to do, what the women were even *like* [in San Francisco]," she remembers.

"I went into the bookstores, and I looked for a magazine [that would give me that information]—I thought, 'Of course, there should be *one.*' I asked around and [I was told], 'Nope. Nothing like that.' I called my best friend in Washington, D.C., and I said, 'This is ridiculous!' [And my friend said,] 'Well, I don't see what you're complaining about; there's nothing here, either.' So I thought, hmm, someone should start a magazine like that."

But although Franco eventually became that "someone," it wasn't until a few years later that she decided to create the magazine she thought should exist for lesbians. "I worked in [the gay bookstore] A Different Light, and I was completely out at the time—my whole life had changed about a hundred and eighty degrees—and the first week I worked there, there must have been about twenty women who came in and asked for a magazine like what I had envisioned. I thought, there's a real need for this.

"So I bought about forty books on publishing. I didn't really in my heart believe that I could do it, but I did some research, and I found out what [publishing a magazine] needed."

One thing it needed was money, and that was a problem. As Franco explains, "When I left my marriage, I had my clothes, and that was it. I didn't have any money. Not a dime. Well, a hundred and eighty-two dollars. And a car payment due. So I started working at three jobs to support myself and to try and keep going to school.

"And every book I read [about publishing a magazine] said, 'You're going to need at least x amount of dollars to get started.' So I thought, okay, that's Goal Number One. I won't start talking to people about it until I have at least three-quarters of my money.

So I did *everything*. *Everything* I could. I worked extra hours at the bookstore, I was waitressing, I was working in a law firm, I was doing motorcycle washes, I promoted clubs, I played the stock market—*everything* that was legal that I could do, I did.

"And then I got to a point where I was building up some financial clout, and my credit was excellent. So I put up a sign at A Different Light that said 'Looking for writers and staff members for a new lesbian magazine' and the phone number." Franco obviously was correct about the need for that "new lesbian magazine": "The first month, I got three hundred calls," she recalls. "It was unbelievable. Women from all over were calling me! I thought, this is really great! So I sent out [flyers] to book-stores in Austin, Texas; New York City; southern California—maybe a dozen [bookstores].

"I got *so much* stuff in [the space of] eight months; it was unbelievable. Women even called me and said, 'Well, I don't really have any skills, but if you need any help with answering phones or whatever, let me know; I just think it's a great thing, what you're trying to do.' "

With such encouragement, Franco was ready to turn her vision into a tangible product. And she knew exactly how she wanted this magazine to look. "The one thing I had known when I [started] was the kind of format that I wanted for the magazine; I was so sick of lesbians [being] treated like second-class citizens," Franco declares. "If I was going to do something, I was going to do it so that we were represented as first-class, as having something nice for once. I wanted that thick glossy cover, and I wanted to use nice paper on the inside—something that was recycled *and* can be recycled again.

"We're printed by a lesbian printer; the first issue wasn't, but now we have a lesbian rep who does all of our contracting and puts all the little pieces together. I feel better about giving her my money. We try to do lots of promotion all over the country, and benefits for organizations. I think that any business that claims to be gay or lesbian, and doesn't give back to the community, is going to be in and out just like *that*," Franco exclaims with a clap of her hands.

Although Franco's founding of *Deneuve* was inspired by her search for a San Francisco lesbian magazine, she never intended that this new publication be merely a local venture. "I actually wanted it to be an international magazine," Franco admits, "a force that women from all over could use as a home base. Right now, we're distributed in the continental United States, Hawaii, Alaska, the United Kingdom, Canada, Australia, Puerto Rico; I've got a German account, and a Swedish account.

"We sell about 40 percent [of our issues] in places like Texas and Alabama," Franco relates. "A lot of women in these [areas] don't have any other contact with the lesbian community; we are it."

The young magazine's phenomenal growth is a result both of Franco's talent for promotion and of the grassroots word-of-mouth advertising that has followed *Deneuve* across the country. "Since I was in the club promotion business, I know promotion," Franco explains. "That's something you have to [do], because most lesbians do not set foot *near* gay and lesbian or alternative bookstores. And if you don't get the word out *somehow.* . . . That's why we do a lot of these parties, because [some] women will go to a dance club once a month, but they won't walk into a bookstore."

When asked whether *Deneuve* has a target audience among lesbians, Franco replies, "Our market? Lesbians. We have such a wide range of people who write for the magazine, and who contribute, and from whom we take input, that I can't pin it down to 'women between the ages of twenty-three and thirty-three,' you know? I don't want it to be that way. I want it to be across the board."

Yet most of *Deneuve's* "cover girls" to date have been attractive, trendily dressed women under forty years of age. And, much to Franco's chagrin, those are the women whom *Deneuve's* readers seem to prefer on their magazine's cover. "The first cover [model] was Katie Brown, our managing editor, and she's [around thirty years old]," Franco relates. "The second cover was two women in their late twenties. And then, we really felt the need—okay, we say we're for everyone, let's go out and prove it! Let's put older women on the cover."

And so the cover of the September/October 1991 issue of *Deneuve* featured one of the subjects of that issue's feature article, "Lesbians Over Sixty." And, recalls Franco, "Financially, that issue was a complete bomb. Women wouldn't even pick up the damn thing!" she continues indignantly. "I was working in the bookstore, seeing this, and thinking that the lesbian community is not any better than the straight community! If you don't put a pretty face on the cover, then you can't get them to digest what's on the inside.

"It was just so aggravating! And it was very hard for me. [For] the next 'letter from the editor,' I wrote so many nasty letters, just to get it out of my system. I wrote, 'You are all ageist; how can we represent everyone when you won't financially support us?' [But I didn't publish it; I was afraid that women] would read it and say, 'Who do you think you are? We don't need this! We know what we like!'

"That [issue] was almost a breaking point for us; we really lost a lot financially on that," Franco admits, but adds, "We did it because we *wanted* to do it. And that's why you produce your own magazine, so you can *do* what you want to do. And do what you think the *women* would want you to do. You can't please everyone, you know?"

And pleasing readers is a demanding job. "I sleep about four hours a night," Franco explains. "You have to be dedicated all the time, 100 percent. You have to keep everybody on the staff motivated; you have to do public relations; you have to do your bookkeeping. I'm sure I do enough work for eight or ten full-time employees."

One bit of relief came with *Deneuve's* 1992 move to offices outside the magazine's original home— Franco's apartment. "It was a great feeling to know that the office is going to be more than three steps from my bedroom," Franco declares. "I'm happy it's moving. I won't feel the desire at two o'clock in the morning to jump up and start writing or doing something. Now, I can go home from work! I don't think that I should feel guilty about going home for five hours—four hours of sleep and dinner! *Deneuve* still is going to dominate my life, but having employees walking in and out of your house, having keys, making themselves coffee. . . ."

Still, paying rent for an office is yet another financial obligation for a fledgling magazine in a shaky economy. Franco herself admits, "This is a depressed market. I had financial advisers warn me *not* to start this right now. But I had it planned, and I was going to do what I wanted to do. And where [other] magazines are failing, *Deneuve* is prospering. It's not enough for me to live on, or to pay my employees; just because we put out a nice product doesn't mean we're rolling in dough."

When asked what it will take for *Deneuve* to continue its growth, Franco states, "I need to capture national advertisers. And it's hard, because *Deneuve* is very picky about who we take on as advertisers. We don't want to do any sex ads—no '900-CUNT' ads—[although] if we sold every full-page ad to sex companies, I'm sure we could make a lot of money.

"It's a hard game to play, because we won't say that we like something when we don't like it. Even if they're going to give us money. I think that's vulgar. [And] we do have a limit on how much of the magazine will be ads, and that's something we set up from day one," Franco adds. "It won't exceed 40 percent, which is the opposite from most magazines. I don't think that women should buy a magazine just to read a bunch of ads. If that's the case, give the thing away for free!

"People think we have a lot of money, because we put out a nice product," Franco states. "I get comments like, 'Oh, if you have so much extra money, why don't you give it to' [a particular cause]. And I think, how many times have I gone to my mailbox, and I have a bill to pay the next day, and I'm praying to the lesbian goddess that there's a check in there!

"This [magazine] is my heart, my soul. It will succeed. But if it doesn't—I'm twenty-four years old. You know? And I've been homeless before; three years ago, I was homeless. I lived in my car. I didn't have *any* money. I think I went almost a week without eating anything. Because I'm not the kind of person who would beg. I've worked for everything I have."

Franco's work, and principles, have paid off. *Deneuve*'s first issue sold out in six days. By the time the magazine was six months old, it was featured in a national newsmagazine. The teenager who married her boyfriend because she wanted to "be normal" is now a role model for lesbians all over the country—*and* she has met her "goal to get my office out of my home by the time I'm twenty-five."

And as for Catherine Deneuve:

"If it helps people to remember the name, that is great," Franco declares. "And [in the film *The Hunger*] she *did* play a lesbian vampire scene!"

15.

Toni Armstrong Jr.

Midwife to the Culture: HOT WIRE

In the "About the Writer" notes that accompany her articles and interviews in *HOT WIRE: The Journal of Women's Music and Culture*, Toni Armstrong Jr. frequently refers to her "Type A" personality—a self-description that should come as no surprise to those familiar with Armstrong's resume. While supporting herself as a special education program facilitator and diagnostician in a suburban

The questions and answers on which this chapter is based are contained in a written exchange of letters between Kate Brandt (November 1, 1991, and February 3, 1992) and Toni Armstrong Jr. (March 26, 1992).

Chicago high school, Armstrong supports her lesbian/ feminist community as co-founder, publisher, and managing editor of *HOT WIRE,* for which she also interviews, writes, and photographs. In addition, she compiles *Women's Music Plus: Directory of Resources in Women's Music and Culture,* which lists more than 3,500 creative feminist women and groups. If those things don't keep her busy enough, she is also a hobby-level bass player who has performed with several lesbian/feminist bands, including Surrender Dorothy and the reconstituted Lavender Jane with Alix Dobkin and Kay Gardner.

Asked with which of these many roles she most strongly identifies, however, Armstrong declines to choose one. "I think of myself as a midwife for the emerging women's music and culture baby," she declares. "I have committed and donated all of my talents to this end. It's my life work."

In the late 1970s, while playing bass for such women's groups as the "comedy-punk" Starkissed Tunaband and in a duo with Paula Walowitz, Armstrong also worked as part of a small group of women who published *Paid My Dues: A Journal of Women and Music,* a magazine founded by Dorothy Dean in Milwaukee at the beginning of that decade. At the same time, Armstrong also began producing a directory of women's music resources called *We Shall Go Forth,* later retitled *Women's Music Plus* when she expanded it to include writing and other non-musical cultural resources.

"The idea for *HOT WIRE* took root at the music industry conferences in the mid eighties, where it was clear that there was a desperate need for women working in the feminist cultural industries (music, film/video, writing/publishing, theater, etc.) to share information and resources," Armstrong recalls. She says it was clear to her (as a longtime organizer) that national institutions were needed to support and promote women's music and culture. "The [women's music] festivals have always served this crucial function. *Women's Music Plus* has helped like-minded women find each other, and *HOT WIRE* does its share to break isolation and celebrate our many cultural triumphs," she says.

HOT WIRE was founded in 1984 by Armstrong and "activist and singer Michele Gautreaux; Ann Morris, of Dyke Deck and Artemis Singers fame; and writer Yvonne Zipter," Armstrong recounts. "Our company, Not Just A Stage, put out one edition of *Women's Music Plus*, helped put together the Music Industry Conference in 1984, and also initiated the first National Women's Music Festival Writers Conference. Not Just A Stage broke up after the first issue of *HOT WIRE* [November 1984] due to creative and work-style differences." In 1985, Armstrong created the company Empty Closet Enterprises, the entity that today publishes *HOT WIRE* and *Women's Music Plus*.

HOT WIRE's editorial statement, found in each issue of the magazine, explains that the magazine "specializes in woman-identified music and culture, primarily the performing arts, writing/publishing, and film/video." Armstrong decided early to make *HOT WIRE* a broad-based journal of women's culture rather than a publication devoted exclusively to women's music.

"Even though the rest of the world looks at us as a group, I've always been amazed at how the musicians don't know the writers or the filmmakers, who in turn don't know the theater women or the cartoonists, etcetera," Armstrong says. "Everyone is doing similar woman-identified work, and we are each others' best audiences and supporters, yet we tend to be very isolated from each other. I've always done what I can to facilitate women meeting each other and sharing their work.

"I've heard people say *ad nauseam* that there's no point in preaching to the already converted, but I vigorously disagree," Armstrong comments. "When it comes to women's music and culture, the converted are the ones who are already writing the books, making the films, doing the festivals and concert tours. It is essential that *they* be inspired by the work of other women, that *they* are exposed to other woman-identified visions, so they can continue to grow as artists. We need to be sure the choir hears the music in their souls, so that they can sing loudly enough for new people to hear. It is crucial that we all get validation and applause. Women's cultural workers have a desperate need to be functioning in community, and to have fun with other women— especially during these years where the mainstream media is so determined to demoralize us and invalidate our work."

Armstrong's concern has always been for the growth of the entire woman-identified subculture. "Music and writing are the most developed now, with theater and film/video exploding right behind," she says. "Women's music has so far been the most diverse; you'll see feminist films and hear lesbian writers give lectures at 'women's music festivals,' whereas the writing conferences and the film festivals tend to be more genre-specific. Women's music has come the farthest the fastest, I think."

HOT WIRE's, and Armstrong's, philosophy of inclusiveness extends to the sexual preference of the magazine's subjects and contributors. Although *HOT WIRE*'s content is frequently lesbian in focus, and Armstrong is openly lesbian-identified, the publication itself is not identified as a "lesbian journal."

"This is a key issue, one to which I've devoted years of thought," Armstrong muses. "We are above all *woman-identified*. That's our primary identification, as well as being specifically feminist. Being woman-identified may or may not have anything to do with being lesbian, but it's *always* focused on the female sensibility, and on relationships between females. The specific topic could be mothers and daughters and grandmothers, friends, sisters, the women's movement, lesbian love relationships, the love between women musicians, the relationship a woman has to the world at large, 'the woman in your life is you,' whatever. Being woman-identified means *by, for, and about women*."

Armstrong never misses an opportunity to point out that feminist lesbians have been at the forefront of all aspects of women's music and culture—behind the scenes and in the audiences. "That's just common sense," she says. "We're the ones most likely to be interested in women and in positive representations of women. Unlike our straight sisters, we generally don't have husbands and boyfriends who can't attend women-only events with us. And since women's culture doesn't focus on men, most of the husbands and boyfriends are uninterested in—if not uncomfortable with—our art, even in venues where they *are* welcome to attend. So it's mostly lesbians, bisexual women, and single straight feminists who are willing to spend all their vacation days at a festival, or spend their Saturday nights at a women-only coffeehouse.

"Still," she points out, "although it's predominantly lesbians who are active in women's music and culture, there are *many* women who are bisexual, heterosexual, celibate, confused, previously-lesbian-now-straight; they are feminists who also share our love of things woman-identified. Why shouldn't they be absolutely welcome? They're woman-identified women, and if they're willing to participate in this vibrant, fabulous culture we're creating for ourselves, I want to welcome them with open arms. We live in a fluid world, and need to keep the boundaries firm but with the doors open wide enough to allow entry to those who share our visions."

Like many (if not most) lesbian/feminist publications, *HOT WIRE* is fueled by love and dedication rather than money. "From the beginning, *HOT WIRE* has been run with a volunteer staff, no grant funding of any sort, and minimal ad revenues," Armstrong explains. "We didn't even have a computer for the first few years. It's been an intense struggle to put out a professional product without finances, proper equipment, or paid staff. We do it out of my basement—which is actually a big improvement over our early years of doing it in my living room and kitchen!

"With volunteer organizations, there's usually a steady turnover in personnel, and we're no exception," Armstrong points out. "There are only a handful of us still here from issue number one. We had about a dozen women doing the project when we started back in 1984; now there are more than sixty staff names on our masthead."

The staff writers usually have their own ideas for articles, although Armstrong sometimes asks them to do specific stories. "We accept unsolicited articles, and occasionally have found very talented writers that way, such as Bonnie Morris," she says. "Most often, I approach women to write for us, or to contribute photos and artwork. It's difficult; I have to come with hat in hand each time because we can't really pay. Almost everyone has been very cooperative, though, presumably because they agree with us that *HOT WIRE* is an important vehicle for woman-identified women of every persuasion."

But having an all-volunteer staff doesn't make *HOT WIRE* any less professional in its standards than its mainstream counterparts. "I keep a tight rein on editorial content," Armstrong asserts. "I'm a strict taskmistress when it comes to editing! We've gotten abundant praise for the high quality of the writing over the years, which reinforces my determination to get the *highest possible* quality. Not everyone likes having her work edited, but with each passing year I gain confidence in my own judgment and abilities as an editor, and I feel less queasy about asking for revisions. If the ideas are good, I'll work with any writer to try to salvage something that's badly written. That's a frequent occurrence, because many of our 'writers' are inexperienced— maybe they're musicians, or girlfriends of the musicians, or whatever. Many times I practically have to rewrite the pieces from scratch. Revisions can take up to twelve hours per article."

Such tenacity is typical of Armstrong's dedication to *HOT WIRE.* "I've always felt that I had an ironclad commitment with the universe to keep *HOT WIRE* going for one generation—about ten years—no matter what," she says, adding, "Only once has that vow seriously wavered, and fortunately some other women came forward with emotional support and hardcore advice at the crucial moment. Things have been fine ever since."

Armstrong's crisis of faith occurred during the winter of 1991, when she considered ceasing publication of *HOT WIRE* as a triannual journal. But Armstrong changed her mind after receiving some welcome moral support, confirming her belief in the importance of "validation and applause." In particular, the celebrated political folksinger/actress Ronnie Gilbert and her partner Donna Korones, and Lynn Wenzel of the feminist newspaper *New Directions for Women,* contacted Armstrong and convinced her to continue *HOT WIRE.*

Armstrong's renewed energy and involvement with *HOT WIRE* is reflected in the talent and reputation of the women she has been able to attract to the journal. As she notes enthusiastically, "We're proud of the women who have agreed to appear on our covers [and we're proud of] the names on our masthead. A quick read-through shows that *HOT WIRE* has effectively become a catalyst for some of the most talented lesbians and feminists of our generation, including writers, photographers, and graphic artists. We're already an impressive and diverse group. I believe women of the future will look back and think, 'If only I could have been there *then*!'—sort of the way we romanticize Paris in the twenties."

Armstrong doesn't like the way the women's community is portrayed in the media—both mainstream and alternative. "As a community, we often get a bum rap for being divisive and fragmented; *HOT WIRE* disproves that sorry old myth and shows that all kinds of women *can* in fact come together for a common goal and sustain the effort, without men and without much money," she says.

Although Armstrong may substitute "the occasional nap" for a good night's sleep and admits that some years she donated more per month for *HOT WIRE* than she was paying in rent, she knows the importance of a magazine like *HOT WIRE* to the women's culture movement, especially when compared to the mainstream press or even to what she calls the "non-feminist gay press." Armstrong says of the latter, "Women's music is almost universally dismissed as a bunch of white girls with guitars, or else we are hit over the head with how the whole thing is 'dead.' It drives me nuts. To read some of these publications, you'd think 'the new lesbianism' is women sleeping with men, or being put to sleep with that 'boring old women's music.' Most of the writers and editors who are involved in printing the women's-music-is-dead articles really have very little exposure to the real-life women's music and culture scene, so it's *especially destructive* for them to print such negative, one-sided commentary. They don't even have the facts."

But Toni Armstrong Jr. does, and she's used her knowledge and passion to help make women's music and culture the broad-based and influential phenomenon it has become over the last twenty years. For Armstrong, as well as for her colleagues and readers, "women's music" is more than a collection of records, just as *HOT WIRE* is more than a mere magazine. As Armstrong declares: "A lot of effort has to be expended in the struggle to end oppression, but our real triumph is that we are managing to fight *and at the same time* create artistic beauty and joyful expressions of our lives. They can oppress us, but as long as the flame of creativity burns brightly, we are winning."

16.

Lisbet

Inventing Aché: *A Journal for Lesbians of African Descent*

Lisbet wants to be clear about something.

"I'm *not* a writer," she declares. "I'm an info-phile, if you will." Lisbet is explaining how she became the founding editor and publisher of *Aché*, a San Francisco Bay Area–based quarterly publication billed as "A Journal for Lesbians of African Descent." "I had some friends who lived in New York, and we were always in the process of circulating information back and forth," she begins. "We were talking about

Interview conducted May 8, 1991.

putting together what started as [something similar to] the Gay [Yellow] Pages, but for Black women."

So in February 1989, with her friend Pippa Fleming, Lisbet "started to gather different bits of information. Then we also saw the need for some sort of coordinated event listing. It just grew into more and more ideas for resources. And the more we thought about it, we dreamed all these things, like 'We could do this!' and 'We could do that!' When we started, it was pretty much based around a calendar of events, and trying to put together a bulletin board where women could talk to each other, because there wasn't a whole lot of cohesiveness outside of just cliques of friends.

"And it really grew!" Lisbet exclaims. "We asked for submissions, and pretty much recruited works from our friends. Then the more poetry, the more fiction, the more journal-type entries we got, [*Aché*] started to form itself. And by the third issue, the community started to respond with all these different things. My amazement was that every issue, it became something different, just simply by what someone would send in."

One facet of *Aché*'s constant metamorphosis is the culture-specific manner in which Lisbet gathered material for the journal. "In the beginning, it was totally solicited effort," she remembers. "I would be sitting there and I'd have eight pages [of articles], and I'd be going 'Help!' I'd get on the phone and call people who I knew were writers, and say, 'Do you have anything you'd like to submit?' or try to commission them to do some piece on something.

"But also, from the beginning, we were really

172

committed to the Black lesbian community, and there's a certain segment of our community that would never write or submit anything to a journal, or come out on any kind of level. So we would take a tape recorder and go into the bars. We had a section [in the magazine], 'On the Table,' where we'd have a topic question. We would actually go to where people were, and talk to them, and record and transcribe it.

"I, for one, would never write and submit anything; that's not something that comes easily and is natural for me to do," Lisbet admits. "Whereas I will talk, and if someone cared enough about what I had to say to go out there and get it, then I would certainly add my two cents worth.

"Now that the journal is more widely known, there are a lot of writers who see it as a place to get their work published. But I think side-by-side there are also the women who have never done anything like that before, and just have something to say."

Aché's growth has resulted in some structural changes. Most notably, after two years as editor/ publisher, Lisbet decided in 1991 to give up her editorial duties and to continue with the magazine "only" as publisher and fundraiser. "*Aché* first started as a personal project," Lisbet explains. "It was something [Pippa and I] could do; it was manageable, it wouldn't cost a lot of money, and we could handle it ourselves. [But] very quickly, it just grew. When we [first] sat down and had a brainstorming session of all the things that *Aché* could be—it got there in three or four months, where there were people all across the country wanting it. Very quickly, it grew into much more than I could handle.

"And, after six months, Pippa left. So I was producing this forty-page publication and financing it all by myself! It was too much. If we had foreseen it growing into this, we would have organized it much differently from the beginning. But it was always a smaller project, something we could do ourselves in our free time. So I found myself in the classic position of having to build a structure around something that was basically structureless.

"I feel like I learned a lot through *Aché*," Lisbet reflects. "I started [out] knowing absolutely nothing. I've never had any sort of formal training [in publishing], and I pretty much learned as I went. There are women out there who *have* skills in publishing and editing, who can take the journal further, to where it needs to be."

Assembling the group that eventually became the first editorial staff of *Aché* happened as a direct result of the journal's policy of publishing women who had "something to say," whether or not they were polished or professional writers. "The production [of *Aché*] was something that I was handling reasonably well," Lisbet recalls. "[But] I was dealing mainly with writers who had never before been published, so each piece was very traumatic. Every time somebody puts their writing out, it requires a lot. Every issue might have maybe twenty different writers, and every one of them would need to be talked through this, and helped with that, and didn't know how to word this—and I was doing that all myself.

"So the people who were regular contributors, who came back time and time again—I started to solicit their help. As they were getting skills, I would start to have *them* work with new writers. At some point, I called a meeting with the women who had been fairly steadily contributing, either with their work or with their time or donations, and I just said, 'This is where it's at: *Aché* is going to die unless we really organize behind it.' And the women who were committed to seeing that it survived, stayed. And most of them are still here."

DeeAnne Davis, who became senior editor of *Aché* in April 1991, "was working with me and seeing what the process was," Lisbet recalls. "She's trained as an editor, and she had a lot of ideas [about] different things that [we clearly] needed, [including] many more people than we currently had. There were things that had been in the journal for quite some time that needed to be developed—the bulletin board wasn't reaching its potential, the calendar was inconsistent—and we discussed the need for having people in charge of each section and developing each section."

The new editors took over *Aché* for the April/May 1991 issue, with an unusual proviso, published in that issue: "We, there are nine of us, are committed to a year of developing the journal—adding our 2 cents. Then we hope to hand over the job to another set of energetic, creative sisters to carry the torch and expand upon our accomplishments."

Lisbet explains, "Actually, I should say that, rather than having a whole new house come in [after a year], [the editors] are committed to their posts for a year, and will evaluate [their commitments] at that time. What we found was that, to take on a section, we needed to have a year's commitment from people. Because, given the nature of our community, there are a lot of people who just can't make commitments for a long time for something for which they're not getting paid. So, I would be very surprised if, at the end of the year, everybody just walked away; but I wouldn't be surprised if people gave up being in charge of certain things, and just took a more peripheral role."

Indeed, starting with the April/May 1992 issue, former features editor Natalie Devora replaced DeeAnne Davis as senior editor of *Aché*. Three editors from the 1991–1992 staff stayed on, and six new editors joined the staff.

But Lisbet remains an important part of *Aché*. "I still do some of the production work, and I handle getting it to the [printer], and basically raise the money for it," she explains. "I'm the head of the Fundraising Committee and the Events Committee; I've got plenty to do."

The fundraising and events that Lisbet conceives and coordinates are done in the name of the organization Aché, which in early 1992 was incorporated as a nonprofit group called The Aché Project, consisting of Fundraising, Outreach, Events and Volunteers, and Journal committees. However, Aché, the organization, does not exist specifically to support *Aché*, the journal.

"No one thing supports the journal financially, I have to say," Lisbet admits. "Subscriptions and donations cover a percentage of the journal costs at this point. We've gotten a couple of grants, but the first was an organizational development grant that doesn't fund publications, and the other was specifically to set up an office. So, technically, the journal itself is funded by the community for which it's published.

"We try and have events, but the events don't really make that much money, either!" Lisbet laughs ruefully. "So, while everything began with the journal, the organization is really developing alongside the journal. And it serves more of its own purpose as opposed to just supporting the journal. We're looking into funding that will cover journal production. We're also looking to a major donor campaign to get a printing press, which would change everything. But, in the meantime . . ."

The "meantime" includes a lot of plans for *Aché's* growth. One indication of the vision Lisbet has for *Aché* is the change in its subtitle, from "The Bay Area's Journal for Black Lesbians" to "A Journal for Lesbians of African Descent." Is there a long-range plan to make a transition to a publication of national interest?

"We've been talking about that for a long time," Lisbet replies. "It's really a function of getting our publication known and out there, and also of fine-tuning the production process—getting the journal running smoothly. At this point, we can't print a lot of copies, so they can only go so far. We don't have a lot of resources to do a lot of advertising, but for the resources that we do have, our network is growing dramatically. We've done work with organizations all across the country.

"My particular vision for *Aché* is not so much a journalistic effort—for example, to do current events," Lisbet explains. "Even though we do cover current issues, such as conference reports, I feel that there are other publications that can do that better, like *BLK* [a Los Angeles–based Black gay periodical]. With their resources, they can do much more. I feel that what *Aché* is, is more of a journal. It deals with things that are not necessarily time-oriented or geographically oriented. It's much more giving voice to people who haven't really had a space for that, and also giving voice to people who don't necessarily have traditional writing experience and skills.

"I really love the journal," Lisbet declares. "It is really satisfying to me. For example, I'd be typing [a transcript], somebody talking about how they felt as a kid—being different, being alone—and then I'd realize, 'This woman is saying what 99 percent of us have felt!' Here is a woman who doesn't write, talking from the heart about something that every one of us will relate to.

"*Aché* is not a newspaper; it's not *Essence* magazine," Lisbet laughs, comparing her journal to the mainstream Black women's magazine. "It's 'something else,' period. That [growing-up] piece can run side-by-side with something on Katherine Dunham, or a conference—I love the diversity."

As part of this diversity, and despite its self-description as a "Journal for Lesbians of African Descent," *Aché* does not restrict its audience to the Black lesbian community. The magazine's editorial statement characterizes the journal as one published "by lesbians of African descent for the benefit of all Black women."

"From the beginning, we felt that it was very important that one of the main functions of *Aché* be to increase the visibility of lesbians in the Black community," Lisbet explains. "It's the type of thing where we've always been there, but we've never been out. So we felt it was very important, on the front page, to say quite clearly who we were. We feel that a lot of the work that we do is dealing with bridging the gaps: between other women, with the Black community. We talk about a lot of different things. And we have quite a few straight women who subscribe to our publication, and even contribute to it on some level."

Aché's place in its home communities is something about which Lisbet is passionate. "I remember when I was first discovering women's bookstores," she recalls. "There were a few [African American lesbian] books—for example, I found *Home Girls: A Black Feminist Anthology* [edited by Barbara Smith], and for me, that was the beginning; it profoundly changed my life! There were a few writers out there whose work you could find—Pat Parker, Audre Lorde—and from there, it started you on your path.

"And I look at where we are now, ten or fifteen years later; there's such a wealth. [With younger Black lesbians,] whether or not they read *Aché*, at least *Aché* is there. There is a publication *for* them; there *is* something there, when they choose to [read it], *for* Black lesbians! I don't know how long *Aché* will last," Lisbet reflects, "but I'm certainly doing whatever I can to make sure that there will be enough of it around that it won't be that hard to find."

With her tireless vision and her enthusiastic dreams for the future ("I would *love* to publish some books; I know *tons* of ass-kickin', dynamic, cutting-edge, straight-up wonderful writers who need to be published—and the sound of 'Aché Press' just makes the hair on my legs stand straight up!"), Lisbet and her *Aché* offspring fortunately should never be "hard to find."

III.
LESBIAN WRITERS
TALK ABOUT
THEIR PASSIONS

No More Ivory Towers:
Art and Politics

Jewelle Gomez

Minnie Bruce Pratt

Sarah Schulman

17.

Jewelle Gomez

"I Feel Powerfully Connected to the Struggles"

Jewelle Gomez initially thought that the reason she had trouble writing when she was a young woman was that she had no role models. "I would want to be a writer, and I would think of myself as growing up to be a writer," Gomez recalls. "[But] I would sit down with a piece of paper and have no clue as to what I could write about, since I didn't really know any Black women writers."

That situation changed in the 1970s when Gomez

Interview conducted October 26, 1991.

first saw a performance of Ntozake Shange's "choreo-poem" *for colored girls who have considered suicide/when the rainbow is enuf.* "When that [play] was first performed," Gomez reflects, "I realized that the reason I had been so blocked was *not* just that I didn't have a role model for Black women writers; [it was] that I really wanted to write about women, and my life as a woman, and there wasn't very much of that out there. Any time you saw anything that had strong women characters, it was talked about as if it was really about the men—like *A Raisin in the Sun,* by Lorraine Hansberry. So it was seeing a play that was really about women that made me know that that's what I was going to do, and really commit myself to doing it."

Gomez was inspired by this experience not only to write her first collection of poetry, *The Lipstick Papers,* but also to self-publish it. "I saved up the money, got somebody to help me design the cover and set it out in type, and that book did really well," she relates. "And I was able to *read* my work *for* people; I liked doing that. From then on, I thought of myself as a writer. Once I had a *book* and I was able to say the words out loud in front of people, I thought I was a writer," Gomez laughs.

But the foundation for Gomez's writing about women's lives was established even before her encounter with *for colored girls.* Gomez's matriarchal family—her great-grandmother, grandmother, and mother, about whom she has written frequently—provided "many and varied influences," according to Gomez.

"My great-grandmother and grandmother were both great readers," Gomez recalls. "So I got my sense of literature from them. And they were indiscriminate readers. Whatever they read got passed on to the next one; my grandmother would pass it on to my mother, if I didn't grab it. It could be anything from *The Fall of the Roman Empire* to James Cain—I mean, just really everything.

"I read [each book], and if I was too young to understand it, I would let it pass on and I'd get the next one!" Gomez remembers with a laugh. "When I think about it, it's just so wonderful, because reading was such a big part of [these women's] lives. These were not women with big educations, but they understood the power of imagination. And that was a major factor in my wanting to be a writer. That, and their storytelling ability.

"My grandmother *loved* to tell stories; she and my mother used to sometimes get together and tell stories about things that happened when they were younger. And my father was a great storyteller, too. He was a bartender, and he was just a hilariously funny guy, and I *loved* being able to take in this big world through him.

"So those are the things, really, that influenced my writing, influenced me to *be* a writer, and gave me a sense of the world as a bigger place than the narrow confines of the tenement building and the disarray of the poor neighborhood that I lived in—all those really oppressive things that would conspire to keep me from thinking of myself as creative or imaginative."

Creativity and imagination are two qualities found in abundance in Gomez's work today. "I don't think that writing is meant to make you feel necessarily comfortable," she explains. "It's much

187

more interesting if writing can stretch you. That's one of the reasons I like to write fantasy fiction, because I can reconfigure the universe in interesting ways that can be challenging."

"Interesting" and "challenging" are understatements when applied to Gomez's Lambda Literary Award-winning first novel, *The Gilda Stories*. *Gilda*'s title character is a Black lesbian vampire whose adventures during the years 1850 to 2050 include working as a servant girl in a New Orleans bordello (where she "exchanges blood" for the first time), owning a beauty parlor in Boston, and performing as a jazz singer in New York City, until, finally, she is the object of a desperate hunt in an environmentally desolate Southwest of the future for her ability to give eternal life.

"In *Gilda*, I first had to [reconfigure the universe] by reshaping vampire mythology: by stripping away the traditional vampire ideas and trying to recreate something that was much more in keeping with my feminist ideology," Gomez explains. For example, Gilda is taught that when she takes blood, she must give something back. And so Gilda looks into the thoughts of the people who give her life, and in exchange for their blood gives them dreams or hopes or solutions to problems.

"By the same token, though, I could not abstract my characters from [the] reality that I was portraying," Gomez continues. "So, although the book has a feminist grounding, it does not have a pacifist grounding. My character lives through very violent times—since [the book] starts in 1850!—and I want to reflect that. Creating a character who does reflect her anger, her bitterness—even times when she does resort to violence and regrets it—is for me a way to push other women to think about the kind of anger that maybe they think they've grown past, or never even experienced."

Another objective for Gomez in writing *Gilda* was to create "a positive Black male character. I feel very connected to Black men in this culture, because of history, and haven't totally given up on them. So I consciously worked on a character.

"And I decided that I didn't want the character to be a namby-pamby Black guy that every woman would love." Gomez laughs. "I wanted to create a *real character,* which is a man who's been shaped by the patriarchy, who thinks that if he likes a woman, it means he should sleep with her. And I needed to create that kind of character who could then learn *better.* That was important to me, because I wanted women and men to see the potential when people are able to shed [old ways]—what good things can happen."

While this character, Julius, does not have a sexual relationship with Gilda, other characters do, and Gomez explains, "The sexuality [in the book] is another way that I attempt to stretch people's imaginations a little bit. In one of the scenes, Gilda is reunited with the woman who helped change her into a vampire, who has been kind of a mother figure for her. And in their reunion, in which they do exchange blood again, I really tried to make it erotic *and* maternal at the same time, because I was interested in the sensual feeling of any kind of physical union.

"And that includes maternal feeling; I mean, a child suckling at a woman's breast is a very sensual feeling," Gomez asserts. "I wanted to be able to recreate that in a way that might be a little startling to people. It's scary, because am I implying incest? Well, no, I'm not; I'm implying that there is a physical sensation that we can appreciate in almost any connection.

"It was interesting to write it," Gomez notes with a laugh, "and [try to] figure out, well, hmm, wonder if people will stop speaking to me? And that was exciting to me. Any writing that uses sexuality, or sensuality, is an easy way to 'push people's envelopes'! Because most of us have such very narrow ideas about what is and isn't appropriate sexually. So doing anything sexual [in writing] is definitely a way to get people to stop and think about what's going on."

Most of Gomez's work over the years has had the intent—and result—of "[getting] people to stop and think about what's going on." For example, Gomez has written about right-wing censorship of art with gay and sexual themes, noting that lesbians and gay men have courageously added this fight to those against AIDS, gay-bashing, and other threats to our community.

When asked why we should fight for art when our physical survival is so often at stake—whether, in fact, we should solve other problems first and then fight from a position of power—Gomez replies, "My sense of what survival is about is that all those things are connected. One cannot presume that you can go at your physical survival hammer and claw, and that every other aspect of your life will remain the same, and that once you physically survive, you can take up [those other aspects].

"Yes, I feel a commitment to fighting against racism in this country. But it is not disconnected from the fight against homophobia. It *can't* be, for me, *personally*, being both Black and a lesbian. I can't *prioritize* which is a worse oppression. I am aware that they're interconnected. And I think that *more* people have to see that, and begin to understand politically how connected the ethos that allows racism is to the ethos that allows homophobia or anti-Semitism or ableism."

Concerning her role as an artist, Gomez reflects, "For me, as a writer, I feel *powerfully* connected to the struggles. I mean, there's nothing really particularly activist in *Gilda*, but it grows out of the political commitment that I have, and I want it to reflect that. If I were writing about anything, as an artist who has a political consciousness, I would think [the work would have] a political perspective.

"And I think that's very important. Because *most* of the people in our world are *never* going to be political activists. I don't care *how* many people you see out there marching on Gay Pride Day; you can always presume that there are at least ten times that many somewhere at home, reading the Sunday newspaper!" Gomez exclaims.

"Art and culture—in the sense of entertainment; I'm not talking about some political high ideal—are the things that people will *always* turn to. And it *is* important for us to protect our right to [exist]—in print, as well as in medical care. Those things are *not* separate; they're not separate at all."

But, as Gomez points out, "[The right wing] relies on people saying, 'Well, no, we need more schoolbooks; we can't have you people giving money to artists!' I would be *much* happier if people would be able to say, 'Why are you giving a parade for the returning Desert Storm troopers, and spending all that money—why don't [you] donate some of that money to the school system?' *That's* where the question should be; it's not, why are we giving money to artists when we need schools. Because all those things are interconnected: the artists and the education and the health—it's all connected."

Gomez has had an additional opportunity to put her beliefs into practice since her appointment in 1990 as director of the literature program at the New York State Council on the Arts (the agency where she had worked for the previous eight years). "In my head was never the idea that I wanted to be the director of the literature program," Gomez relates. "All I wanted to do was have a regular job that would pay me and not get on my nerves, so I could write. And that's what the job did. [But] in the eight years being there, I learned a lot about the field: the kind of things you can do to expand the perspective of the traditional literary milieu, which is relatively narrow and conservative, even the ones who think of themselves as progressive.

"And I realized that I really *wanted* the job [as director]," Gomez admits. "I wanted it. And I realized that I wanted it because it *does* have deep significance in these times. For someone who is actively 'out' as a lesbian—I mean, there are a lot of gay people working in the agency, but few are politically *active*.

"It feels wonderful to be 'out,' because it means that the traditional literary folk cannot make any presumptions when they come to me. And most of the people who do small press books and magazines, and reading series around the country, are really interested in being a part of the mainstream, even though they like to think of themselves as being the avant garde. They're just really looking for a piece of the same pie; they're not interested in changing that perspective, in being more inclusive. They give very good lip service to it, because they've come out of a liberal tradition, but they're really not [inclusive].

"And it's very exciting to know that when I call up and ask a question, they know they're talking to a Black woman, and there's *only* so much B.S. that they can give me!" Gomez laughs. "It's also exciting because I know that my name is known enough in the world that if a lesbian or gay group or writer wants to know something about our program, they'll call me, which they might not have [done] in other times. And that feels good. I will go out of my way to *look* for Black organizations, or Black writers, or lesbian and gay writers. And that's very exciting, that I have a better chance of finding them, you know?

"For me personally, this is a stunning turn of events," Gomez reflects. "I grew up with my great-grandmother, who had very little education, although she was very smart. When I graduated from high school, my *mother* hadn't graduated from high school; she since has. So for me to have my career culminate in this kind of thing is personally very—I mean, it's just moving to me."

Gomez notes about her great-grandmother, "Her sense of history and her perspective gave me a very strong sense of my connection to the past, and, I think, because of that, an interest in my connection to the future." And Jewelle Gomez, by means of her tradition-challenging fiction, her powerful and angry essays, and her breaking down of the old restrictive barriers defining "literature," has built on that connection to the past and helped create a future in which those who never were allowed to speak finally will be heard.

Works by Jewelle Gomez: *The Gilda Stories* (Firebrand Books, 1991); *The Lipstick Papers* (Grace Publications, 1980); *Flamingoes and Bears* (Grace Publications, 1986)

18.

Minnie Bruce Pratt

Standing Up to the Literary Academy

Minnie Bruce Pratt didn't start writing poetry until she was a college freshman, but she soon discovered that she "*loved* the writing" that she was doing. In the years since, Pratt has published five volumes of poetry and prose, winning awards, grants, recognition, and admiration in the process.

But Pratt admits that, in her student writing days, "I absolutely never thought that I would be a writer. I thought of myself as a woman who was going to have to earn her living. My mother had

Interview conducted June 10, 1991.

been the economic mainstay of our family, and I just knew that I was going to have to have a—I don't even know that I thought of it exactly as a career—I decided I was going to go on and get a Ph.D. and teach."

This decision was reinforced by "some very clear messages I was getting from the people who were my mentors," as Pratt recalls—especially after she married. "I can remember my philosophy professor at a party after our wedding, sitting on the couch and saying, 'All right, Minnie Bruce, you're going to be the scholar and'—pointing to my husband, saying—'and you're going to be the poet.' We were both writing poetry, but everybody was very concerned that we get our roles clear.

"So, in fact, I did stop writing. And I didn't start again until I fell in love with another woman, and I immediately started writing poetry again!" Pratt laughs. "Immediately. Not love poetry, just—I just started writing. About what was going on. That was in 1976. So I didn't write for over ten years. And then I started again. And I haven't stopped since then."

In spite of her return to writing, however, Pratt admits that "it took me a long, long time after I started writing to begin to be able to call myself a writer. I'd been writing for five or six years pretty seriously before I could start calling myself a writer, and then it took longer to call myself a poet."

What made Pratt finally able to identify herself as a poet? "Just doing it. Just continuing. I just kept writing. And I was working on a literary magazine, *Feminary,* so I was with other people who were serious about writing, and about politics, and about being lesbians. Then I would travel, mostly because of *Feminary*, and I would meet other people. I went to a National Women's Studies Conference, and they seemed completely prepared to take me seriously!"

Pratt laughs at this recollection, but then reflects, "It was because there was a culture of lesbians writing. Other people were taking lesbian writing seriously. Harriet Desmoines [now Ellenberger] and Catherine Nicholson [founding editors of the lesbian journal *Sinister Wisdom*] were in Charlotte, North Carolina, when I was in Fayetteville, North Carolina. They were editing *Sinister Wisdom* from there, and I got to know them. They arranged to have me invited to do a poetry reading with some other people in Charlotte. That was the first time I ever did a poetry reading, and the first time I was ever publicly out as a lesbian, also. Eventually, some folks wanted to publish my work. People were saying, 'Do something with it. Send it. Do readings.'

"I feel very keenly that I'm not sure I would have been able to have come back to my writing if there hadn't been this movement—gay and lesbian movement, women's liberation movement, and lesbian cultural movement—if there hadn't been those movements, I don't know that I would have done any serious writing. I think I really feel like I'm the product of the work of a lot of other people, that my work really comes out of that matrix, very very much so."

Because Pratt's roots as a writer are grounded in these various liberation movements, and because of the changes in her life that led her to begin writing after a long silence, she declares, when asked if she considers her poetry to be political, "Oh, absolutely!

Absolutely. My poetry was *always* political. Partly because I started writing it out of my personal circumstances, which were *completely* political," she laughs.

"You know: I came out, I immediately got into conflict with the man I was married to about that, and began to struggle about the children. I had enough awareness, because I had gotten to know women, *and* women who were lesbians, who were involved in women's liberation, and I had had enough conversation with them, and they had given me enough information, that I *had* a political analysis about what was happening to me. So that that immediately informed and shaped what kind of poetry came out of that experience.

"I started writing poetry to survive, emotionally and mentally and physically, during that time. But it was, again, very much shaped by the political context of the women's movement and lesbian culture."

The poems that Pratt wrote about her coming out, and especially about her subsequent loss of custody of her two young sons, eventually were collected in a volume titled *Crime Against Nature*. Although these powerful poems are extremely personal, and about a very painful time in her life, "I never thought that I *wouldn't* publish them," states Pratt. "Ever since pretty early on in my writing, I never thought about not publishing things, even when they were quite personal. Again, this is very connected to my idea of how poetry functions in a political context and in the building of communities and the building of liberation efforts. It's part of not staying hidden about things; only if we make the struggles that we're going through public—only if we move them out of this private arena of torture and pain into some kind of public space—can there be public change.

"What was more problematic was writing them!" Pratt recalls with a laugh. "But once they were coming, and I could see that I had quite a substantial body of poems around this experience, then it just never occurred to me that they wouldn't be a book. Never."

Crime Against Nature went on to win great acclaim for Pratt, including a 1989 Lamont Award, an honor given by the Academy of American Poets for a poet's second book. But Pratt's award, prestigious though it is, might never have been noted outside poetry and academic circles had it not been for her acceptance speech. In her talk, Pratt noted that, as a lesbian, she still could be regarded as a criminal in her hometown of Washington, D.C. She also publicly credited the women's and gay and lesbian liberation movements for inspiring her life, her politics, and her work.

While Pratt's words delighted much of her audience (and, later, the larger lesbian and gay community, as word of her brave and eloquent speech became widespread), they apparently shocked the two chancellors of the Academy of American Poets who sat on stage during the acceptance speeches. These men tried to cut off Pratt's speech before she had finished talking by interrupting her and by passing her a note. Pratt, however, continued speaking and reading from her award-winning poetry, as audience members vocally expressed their displeasure at the chancellors' rudeness.

When asked why she chose to give such an explicitly political speech at the award ceremony, Pratt explains, "I felt like, this award is taking me out of my usual context, my cultural/political context, and moving me—for the evening at least!—to the front of the stage in mainstream literary life. And I know how typical it is, in that situation, for the folks in the mainstream to see the person who is the 'minority' as an aberration, or as a dancing dog, or sort of an individual talent, right? Who somehow managed to overcome this disability of her minority status and actually write good poetry.

"I was determined to bring my context with me. And for [the mainstream] to experience me as much as possible within my own culture. And the only way I could do that was to talk about where I had come from, so that they didn't delude themselves into thinking I was rising like Venus on the half-shell out of the ocean," she laughs. "You know? Miraculously standing in front of them with this book that appeared out of nowhere!

"I felt it was really important, *and* I knew that there were going to be people there who had made the culture that I had come from. [Publisher] Nancy Bereano was there, [writers] Barbara Smith, Jewelle Gomez, Judith McDaniel, Adrienne Rich, Marilyn Hacker, Joy Harjo, Elly Bulkin, [photographer] Joan E. Biren [JEB], my sons—you know, I asked a lot of people to come. Plus, there were other people who weren't literary people, but who were significant movement folks.

"And I just thought, am I going to get up in front of these people and act like I just stepped on the stage—again—out of nowhere? No! It wouldn't have been *courteous,* it wouldn't have been *respectful,* it wouldn't have been *accurate.* So, [the speech] upset folks, but—too bad."

Yet Pratt admits that she hadn't anticipated the hostile reaction of the academy chancellors, who, she says, "clearly had *never* read these poems. That was the *irony* of it! They were being hostile to me for the very thoughts and behavior that had enabled me to write the book that [the academy was] giving me an award for.

"They just weren't in touch with what the work was about. They really didn't care. They'd never heard of me; they just didn't care. And that was the thing that was most shocking to me, actually, about the whole evening. The homophobia was horrible. But what was *shocking* to me was the lack of passion about poetry. I'm used to folks taking it seriously. It is about *life.* It is about *living.* It is about the World Out There beyond the walls of the Guggenheim. And I was shocked at the insularity and the narrowness of their feelings about poetry."

While winning an award like the Lamont frequently is an entree to professional advancement, Pratt has found her subsequent fame to be based more in the lesbian and gay community than in mainstream literary or academic circles. "Mostly what's happened is that wonderful gay and lesbian people, who read about the ceremony, have organized to have me come to read at their schools," Pratt explains. "It's like my name became recognizable to people because of the Lamont ceremony.

"So that has been very interesting to me. And not surprising. I did not think I would become a hot item on the writers' conference circuit. I think there's a lot of homophobia, and [*Crime Against Nature*] is very political. And people [often] don't want to deal with somebody who's out as a lesbian, as I am.

"But, on the other hand, the work has gotten recognition I never thought it would. It got reviewed in the *New York Times;* it won [an award from the Gay and Lesbian Task Force of the] American Library Association. I think it's being ordered by more libraries, and it's going to get into the hands of a few more people. And I'm being rewarded by the gay and lesbian community for taking a stand, you know? I mean, 'reward' in the sense of people wanting me to come and be in their community. And that's a wonderful thing to have happen."

Pratt's willingness to take a stand has gone beyond the Lamont ceremony and the Academy of American Poets. When she, along with sister lesbian writers Audre Lorde and Chrystos, were awarded National Endowment for the Arts (NEA) fellowships, the fundamentalist American Family Association and conservative Senator Jesse Helms "mounted quite a campaign" to harass the three women and the NEA about the grants and "to describe my work as pornography and disgusting," Pratt explains. The grants were not rescinded, and Pratt, Lorde, and Chrystos subsequently shared a Hammett-Hellman Award from the Fund for Free Expression for their courage in the face of the right-wing pressure campaign.

"All of this came out of these poems [in *Crime Against Nature*]," Pratt reflects, adding, "When I was growing up in Alabama, I was really oblivious to the civil rights movement. And I looked back on that time later, and I thought, 'You were just so out of sync with what was going on in your era!' Things were always ten years ahead of me. I thought, well, I'm just always going to be out of step, you know?

"And then suddenly, I'm not out of step anymore!" Pratt laughs. "I'm right in the middle of the controversy of my time, around sexuality, and women's liberation, and gay and lesbian issues. I'm *right in the middle* of it. And it's an amazing feeling. It's a lot easier to have clarity about things that you're at a distance from, and a lot harder to have clarity about history when you're in the middle of it. I'm really working hard at understanding what I'm in the middle of right now."

Part of what Pratt is in the middle of, as always, is her writing and her activism. "As somebody who's done a lot of organizing over the years, I've really learned the difference between saying you want something changed, and the thing actually getting changed," she declares. Despite the fact that she considers her poetry to be political, "Words are not action; words lead to action," she says. "Getting myself to do something always means thinking about it, talking about it, writing about it—it's part of creating a new reality. I just don't think one is ever a substitute for the other.

"[For example], I'm not doing any organizing [now]. And I miss the energy that I get from that kind of work, the kind of hope I get, and I'm trying to figure out what I'm going to do next. I think that that kind of getting-together with other people prevents my writing from falling into despair."

But even when she is "only" writing, the stereotype of the lone writer isolated in her ivory tower is one that will never apply to Minnie Bruce Pratt. "I think we all have stories to tell, and some of us choose to go ahead and make that our life," she notes. "If my poetry can be a way of other folks, feeling the worth of their own stories, I consider that political work."

Works by Minnie Bruce Pratt: *The Sound of One Fork* (Night Heron Press, 1981); *We Say We Love Each Other* (Spinsters/Aunt Lute, 1985; republished by Firebrand Books, 1992); *Crime Against Nature* (Firebrand Books, 1990); *Yours in Struggle: Three Feminist Perspectives on Anti-Semitism and Racism,* co-authored with Elly Bulkin and Barbara Smith (Long Haul Press, 1984; republished by Firebrand Books, 1988); *Rebellion: Essays 1980–1991* (Firebrand Books, 1991)

19.

Sarah Schulman

"I'm There Because I Have Certain Beliefs"

"When I meet people—for example, to do an interview—they usually will comment on how they are surprised that I'm so serious and intellectual," Sarah Schulman offers. "Because from reading the books, they expect a raucous alcoholic or something."

"The books" are Schulman's five novels to date, thought-provoking stories "about being marginal, about being invisible, about getting lost," as she

Interviews conducted February 24, 1990, and February 22, 1992.

describes them. While her central characters are lesbians, her books "are not about coming out. There are a lot of issues that are connected to the characters' lesbianism. But the books are not about transforming into the lesbian identity."

Schulman began her writing career as a journalist, working for the New York City–based feminist newspaper *Womanews*. "I wrote for every issue of *Womanews* for five years," she recalls. "That's where I learned how to write about a community for that same community, which is really challenging. The very people you're writing about are the people reading it, and if they detect some kind of voyeurism or lack of sincerity, they let you know right away.

"Writing for the movement press was all about learning description, listening carefully to what people were saying, trying to detect trends. Also, you have the advantage of seeing your work published right away. It's a really good place to learn how to write."

Schulman's first attempt at fiction became her first published novel, *The Sophie Horowitz Story* (1984), which recounts the adventures of a lesbian journalist who is fascinated with a radical fugitive. "I had interviewed these women who were involved with the infamous Weather Underground Brink's robbery in the early 1980s," Schulman explains about *Sophie's* origins. "And their stories were so incredible to me that I just started having fantasies about them and writing stories about them."

Schulman's second book, *Girls, Visions and Everything* (1986), follows "dyke about town" Lila Futuransky through a summer on New York's Lower

East Side. Of *Girls*, Schulman says, "I was interested in the 'lesbian boyhood,' where a girl places herself in the kind of imaginative adventure fiction that's traditionally reserved for boys. I had identified with these writers like Jack Kerouac, and the only way you could enjoy his books was if you were Jack. If you identified with the women in the book, you couldn't enjoy it. 'Lesbian boyhood' was something that a lot of people have experienced, but it hadn't been articulated in fiction."

Of writing her next novel, *After Delores* (1988), a tale of obsessive love and revenge, Schulman declares, "I was really tired of the lack of total range of emotion in lesbian literature. I made a commitment to myself to show myself in the totality of my humanity, and not to censor feelings out of fear.

"When I toured with that book in 1988, I discovered that, when I went to places where gay people felt safe, like San Francisco, they liked the book. When I went to places where gay people did not feel safe, they felt very threatened by the book, because they were still living with this fear that, if you say that you do bad things and have bad feelings, straight people will use this against you. People will point to it and say, 'See, those people can't have healthy relationships.' It was like that fear of the dominant culture was keeping us from being complete people in our own fiction."

Schulman's most recent book, *Empathy* (1992), "a novel about how homophobia affects the female psychology," is "written in thought sentences," she explains. "So instead of being written in a conventional narrative style, it's written the way a person thinks. It's very loopy, and distracted, and fragmented; different ideas will set off other ideas.

"I allowed myself to work for two years without knowing what it was about," Schulman continues. "I just gave myself full permission to write. And when I finally realized what it was about, I was really glad I had given myself that permission, because what I found out was that I was writing totally from my unconscious. And therefore, it got much deeper, emotionally. So, I'm very, very happy with it."

It was in her fourth novel, *People in Trouble*, that Schulman confronted the subject that has cast the longest shadow on the contemporary gay movement: AIDS. At the time that the book was published in 1990, Schulman explained, "*People in Trouble* was [written] from an incredible need for this community to become activist again." She predicted that the book would be "outdated in three years. Because AIDS fiction is going to change and grow really fast. I think we're going to get to a place where we can write about AIDS in a more sophisticated manner. Because we're just beginning to start to write about AIDS, and we're going to be spending the rest of our lives trying to understand it."

Two years after making this statement, Schulman agrees with her own prediction, saying that "for the people who are having direct experience with AIDS and AIDS activism, *People in Trouble* may be outdated." But Schulman admits that her views on AIDS fiction have changed. "There was an expectation that AIDS would be a transformative experience, a moment of truth," she reflects. "And what I've found is that it's *not* true; people do *not* get transformed by having AIDS. They simply become themselves, just ever so much more so.

"And AIDS fiction—there was, I think, a burden placed on it where people expected the writers to have incredible insights into life and death, when actually the opposite has turned out to be true. AIDS fiction has become writing by people who don't feel well, who are depressed, who are writing against the clock and can't put as much time into it as they would like. And so a lot of the work has become rushed, incomplete, unsatisfying. What I'm realizing is that, instead of being revelatory, it's actually restricted. That's what AIDS fiction is, at this point: work in the face of enormous obstacles."

Schulman sees her own writing of AIDS fiction as changed by factors that have evolved with the passage of time. "In *Empathy*, AIDS is treated very differently than it is in *People in Trouble*," Schulman points out, "because in my own life it's become normal. The experience of having someone talk to you about his impending death is now a normal experience that I have all the time. When I was writing *People in Trouble*, I was so shocked.

"I also did not anticipate how fully the government would try to obstruct every single action that people tried to initiate to impact on AIDS. It's been so demoralizing. So I think that demoralization and normalization are now what I'm writing about."

If gay men are not writing about AIDS as richly as was expected a few years ago, lesbian writers are not writing about the plague at all, according to Schulman. "I think lesbian writers are becoming more and more apolitical generally," she says. "I went to the Lambda Literary Awards last year

[1991], and I was really shocked, because every other man who stood up talked about one who had died. And many women stood up and told really empty anecdotes about how they wrote their books.

"The larger world was not present. And I'm not just saying AIDS is the only thing; the collapse of the culture, the crisis of capitalism were not being directly addressed in many cases. Now, on the other hand, I think the quality of lesbian writing is improving," Schulman adds. "There have been some books published that are *excellent,* in terms of literary achievement. But they're not politicized. The lesbian writers are more politically conventional than they've ever been.

"When you take on the responsibility to be a writer, which is to be a public thinker, for a community that is dropping dead, basically, or is under siege—it shocks me that people take that position, to be a public thinker for a community in trouble, and then all they try to provide is entertainment. I don't understand how a person can do that.

"When you walk into a women's bookstore, and look at the lesbian section, most of the books are fairly pallid. They're not engaged with 'The World.' And that's very frustrating to me."

Schulman had her first lesbian relationship when she was sixteen years old, and she describes herself as a member of "the first generation that came out into an already existing gay movement [Schulman was born in 1958]. So when I was a teenager, there were already lesbian novels. *Rubyfruit Jungle* had already been published. This is the first time that we have a group of lesbians who are gay in popular culture, not separated from popular culture.

"Men and women living in both gay culture and popular culture are willingly participating in mixed communities. When I first came out, women's newspapers and organizations were very vibrant places, because there was a lot of discussion going on about how people were going to survive. That discussion is now taking place in a gay and lesbian context. We're seeing, more frequently, a switch to a co-ed community—a community of gay men and women together."

But in the past few years, many younger lesbian activists have become disillusioned working with gay men, and have become frustrated by the racism and sexism that they perceive within some co-gender activist groups. Schulman, a self-described "rank-and-file member of ACT UP," acknowledges the existence of this conflict between lesbians and gay men. "The vast majority of gay men in ACT UP did not have reciprocal relationships with women, politically, socially, or personally," she points out. "And that is not because they're sick and dying, it's because they're men."

But although she admits that "[Most gay men] really don't care about you, except in terms of what you mean to them," such sexism is not enough to discourage Schulman from remaining an activist. "That reality is not enough to determine my decisions about how I behave politically," Schulman says. "Lesbians are involved in every progressive movement for change on the face of the earth. And they don't demand the level of reciprocity in those other movements that they do in the gay movement.

"If I made my political decisions based on who I was going to have an equal relationship with, as a lesbian, I wouldn't be able to work with anyone. So instead, I make decisions based on my own morality and my own political views. There are plenty of men in ACT UP whom I find intolerable, yet somehow I can tolerate them in that context. Because basically we are in agreement in terms of the broader spectrum.

"I've also been frustrated by the inability of lesbians to coalesce politically. If there were a vibrant, activist lesbian movement going on, I'm sure I would want to be part of it, but there isn't. [Schulman has since joined the group Lesbian Avengers, which was founded in September 1992.] My own political belief system determines that I have to be involved where people are organizing. I didn't come to ACT UP because the men like me or don't like me; I'm there because I have certain beliefs."

Schulman's beliefs also have led her to speak out publicly about the controversy engendered during the early 1990s when the National Endowment for the Arts (NEA), pressured by right-wing fundamentalists, repeatedly rescinded or denied grants to allegedly "obscene" artists, many of whom were gay. But while the progressive gay and lesbian community spoke out against this politically motivated censorship, Schulman's protest was unusual in that it focused on her gay and lesbian peers in the arts community as well as on conservatives and the NEA. She addressed race and class issues, and the fact that it traditionally has been white, middle-class artists who have benefited from arts awards.

"[At first], I was the *only* person saying [those things]," Schulman asserts. "And I came under incredible personal pressure to not do that. The whole process was very frightening for me, because I knew that I was isolating myself from people, and I was interfering with people's money, which is really the issue here.

"I recently debated Jennie Livingston [the white director of the documentary *Paris Is Burning*, about poor, young gay men of color and their cross-dressing 'vogue' dance parties] at a benefit," Schulman continues. "I was arguing that what's evolving is this sphere of *official gay culture*, which is gay and lesbian artwork that is promoted and [made a commodity] in the mainstream. The community has to ask if this work is being propelled because it resonates with and represents gay people, or if it is the product of a small sector who, for reasons of class and race, can position themselves strategically.

"Jennie was essentially arguing that if you just work really hard, you can get ahead. And it was interesting, because the audience *really* wanted to believe her. Because her message was that yes, we will be accepted, we will be seen as normal. And my message is, no, we are not normal, we will always be marginalized, and we make a terrible mistake if we buy into this kind of tokenism. I could see people struggling emotionally, but they really couldn't break with the hope of being accepted."

Sarah Schulman may or may not need acceptance of her viewpoint or her work; most artists do, on some level. And few of us are willing to risk losing that acceptance by speaking our consciences when our viewpoint is unpopular. Schulman's tenacious honesty ultimately may be as valuable a contribution to our community as her spirited novels.

Works by Sarah Schulman: *The Sophie Horowitz Story* (The Naiad Press, 1984); *Girls, Visions and Everything* (Seal Press, 1986); *After Delores* (E. P. Dutton, 1988; New American Library, 1989); *People in Trouble* (E. P. Dutton, 1990; New American Library, 1991); *Empathy* (E. P. Dutton, 1992; New American Library, 1993)

The Craft—and Passion—of Writing

Willyce Kim

Lesléa Newman

Terri de la Peña

20.

Willyce Kim

Reluctant Pioneer

Willyce Kim wasted no time in deciding her life's work. "I was about seven years old," she remembers, "and I wrote a baseball story and sent it in to a newspaper contest. I won, and they published [the story] in the paper.

"I guess writing *always* interested me because my dad was a sportswriter," Kim continues. "I was really interested in reading books, and from childhood on, I thought, 'I would like to write.' And I just followed it in grade school and high school."

Interview conducted September 7, 1991.

217

With this head start, Kim was an accomplished poet by the time the lesbian/feminist Women In Print movement took root in the early 1970s. Her desire to publish her work and her interest in lesbian culture led Kim to California's pioneering Women's Press Collective, an early lesbian publisher.

"I met [Women's Press Collective founders] Judy Grahn and Wendy Cadden and Anne Leonard after I had gone to a number of women's dances and poetry readings in the late 1960s or early 1970s," Kim remembers. "I'd seen Judy read at a number of events. I had a manuscript of poems. A Woman's Place bookstore had opened—the original store—and the Women's Press Collective was housed there. So when I [went] to look for books, mainly lesbian material, I had my manuscript, and I turned it in to Judy and Wendy. They liked it, and they were going to publish it. I wanted to be a part of that process, so I joined the Press Collective then.

"I worked with them maybe for four or five years. At that time, we put out [my poetry book] *Eating Artichokes* [1972], and we [reprinted poet] Pat Parker's *Child of Myself.* We put out the first rape pamphlet *ever.* The Press Collective picked up more members during that time; people were coming and going, as people came and went, in those days," Kim remembers with a laugh.

Kim left the Press Collective because "I took a job; I needed money," she recalls. "All that time I'd been working for the Press Collective, and I needed more money, so I left them to get a forty-hour-a-week job. It was hard. Sometimes I'd go back to the press after I got off the job, and I found out I was too tired after [work] to really be committed.

"But looking back on it, it was really incredible to be a part of the beginning stages of the women's press movement, getting out all the lesbian stuff that we could. Now, when I walk [into] a bookstore, it's really thrilling to see all the books. When I originally walked into A Woman's Place bookstore, they had maybe one rack filled with women's poetry, women's prose, lesbian [writing]. Now there's hundreds of books."

Although Kim left the Press Collective, she continued to write. Eventually she wrote two comic novels, *Dancer Dawkins and the California Kid* (1985) and its sequel, *Dead Heat* (1988), picaresque tales of two lesbians' adventures with cults (*Dancer*) and horse racing (*Dead Heat*), not to mention a restaurant owner named Ta Jan the Korean and a talking dog named Killer Shep.

Ironically, though Kim's early writing was published by the ground-breaking Women's Press Collective, she turned to a press owned by a gay man, Sasha Alyson, to publish her novels. "I started writing *Dancer Dawkins* when I had agoraphobia [from which she suffered for two years]," Kim recounts. "I needed some kind of humorous fiction around me; I was reading a lot of it, and I wondered if I could write a book. So that's how I started *Dancer*. And when I finished it, I had no idea who I would go to to publish it. I wanted to go to some press that was looking for more lesbians and that would take care of whoever they published. So I started looking around for gay presses that wanted more women. And Alyson Publications' name came up frequently, so I decided to write them a letter, to see if they were interested. And they were."

But Kim admits that Alyson was not her first choice. "I sent it to Bantam [a mainstream house] originally," she says. "They read the first twenty-five pages and they said, 'Oh, send us more, we're really interested.' They read the next seventy-five pages, and I guess it became too lesbian all of a sudden for them!" Kim laughs. "They said there really wasn't that much of a market! So they rejected it."

Dancer Dawkins and *Dead Heat* differ from more traditional novels in that short vignettes, anywhere from two paragraphs to two pages long, are used instead of longer chapters to tell the story. "I think being a poet inspired me to begin with that format," Kim remarks. "Sometimes I think, when I read a work of fiction, that it's way too wordy, that you could cut to the chase, you could get right down to the bone. I often find [the wordiness] distracting.

"I wanted to write something that would [have] these crystal-clear vignettes of what was happening in each chapter: short, precise—the reader didn't have to wade through a hundred and fifty external pages to get to what was happening. And I think that that's what influences my writing a lot: I think if you give people too much, that's where you lose a lot of readers. So I'd just rather give them what I think is the most important thing—the heart of the matter."

Kim's background as a poet is also evident in the way she titles each chapter. The headings don't always describe the "theme" of the segment; instead, Kim picks one or two words from the narrative to use as her title. "I was a great follower of Bob Dylan," Kim explains, "and a lot of his titles have absolutely nothing to do with what's going on in a song. I think probably that influenced me; I'd look at his titles, and I'd say, 'Wow, what does *that* mean? That has nothing to do with that song he's singing!' I consider him a poet, anyway, so maybe that had something to do with it."

Kim considers herself a poet, as well, despite her success as a novelist. "I was talking to Judy [Grahn] about this one day; we always have nice discussions about writing," Kim recalls. "We both agreed—we both laughed about this—that on our gravestones, more than anything, regardless of how many works of prose [we'd written], we want 'Poet' under our name!"

Kim explains, "To me, I'll probably always be a poet first and somebody who wrote fiction second. Although I *really* enjoy writing fiction a lot—I really do. Both ways of writing are so different, but they're still so rewarding. I just really enjoy doing both of them a lot."

Kim's pleasure in writing is obvious from the whimsical touches she employs in the *Dancer Dawkins* books. For example, one important character is the aforementioned Killer Shep, the talking German shepherd. Kim, who describes herself as "a dog person," explains, "I've always wanted to know, 'Gee, if my dog could only talk, what would the dog say to me?' [If I'm] at work all day, it's too bad I can't come home and ask the dog, 'So, how was your day?' The dog would sit there and say, 'Oh, Miss, I saw x-number of cats and dogs out on the street,' or 'I was really bored today.' So I thought it would be really funny if I had a dog in the book."

Kim laughs as she recounts her talking-dog

fantasy, then explains the context in which a character like Killer Shep places her book as she describes a negative review that *Dancer* received from a feminist newspaper. "[The reviewer] *really ripped Dancer,* because she thought these lesbians should be working," Kim recalls. "[She asked], 'Why didn't I talk about the jobs they had? It seemed like all they did was have this horrendous adventure; weren't these dykes working class?'

"I was really upset, because I think she missed the whole point, that *Dancer* was just a fun book. I mean, how could she rip a book that had a talking dog in it, for God's sake? You know? She wanted a depiction of working-class lesbians, and, hey, my book wasn't it! My book had a talking dog in it! She missed the boat; she ripped the book from front cover to back cover. I thought it was amazing."

But if this particular critic missed the boat, she probably was the only one. In fact, it was because the book's readers asked for more of Dancer and the Kid that Kim wrote a second book about the characters, *Dead Heat.*

"I never thought about [writing a sequel]," Kim admits, "but then I met more and more people who said, 'Do these characters have any more adventures?' And I started thinking, 'Well, maybe they could and maybe they couldn't.' "

Obviously, they could and did. But Kim's current project is a break from Dancer and the Kid's adventures. "It's an erotic love story called *Gabriella,*" Kim explains. "It's something totally different: a serious erotic story. I thought I would try to write one. From humor to eroticism! Then when I tell people that, they [say], 'Aw, no more humorous stuff?' And I think, someday I'll get back to it, but I wanted to write something erotic."

Kim's first attempts to sell *Gabriella* also represented something "totally different" for her: "I decided I would try a literary agent," she recounts. But "he found that it was really hard to move with straight publishers—that's what we were trying to do—and I guess the windows that were open, with the straight publishing houses that had lesbian or gay editors, closed. Different houses got bought, and editors lost their jobs. So I took [the book] back, and I've got it now; I haven't really done anything with it."

In the twenty years that Kim has been publishing her writing, she has seen and experienced widespread changes in the world of lesbian publishing: from groups like the Women's Press Collective, where writers printed and marketed their own work, to more traditionally styled lesbian and gay publishing houses, to mainstream presses and back again. Today, lesbian writers have more options than ever—but do we have less control?

"The major difference, fortunately for all of us, is that there are more [publishing] houses that lesbians can go to," Kim replies. "As far as editorial [control], with Alyson, there was always a dialogue going on. It wasn't, 'Cut this—we don't like it.' A query would come from Alyson, 'What do you think about this?' [or] 'This might be weak.' And you'd write back, 'Oh, I'm not so sure about this; this is the way I feel my character should be doing this.' I never had that pressure, that they were taking total control over my book.

"With the Women's Press Collective, it was a

more subtle editorial sort of thing. When I handed in my manuscript to Judy and Wendy, it wasn't like I handed it to them and they said, 'Okay, we'll publish the whole thing.' They went through it; it was a weeding-out process of, 'Well, this would [be] good with this theme; these poems, as a group, would be the basis of *Eating Artichokes*, these poems maybe something later on.' There was a definite order to the way things got published there."

Anecdotal history tells us that, in early lesbian publishing, "anything" written by a lesbian was printed because it was so important to make lesbian work available. "That's a misconception," Kim says with a laugh at the notion that early lesbian solidarity meant lack of editorial discrimination. " 'Send us your stuff—we'll print anything!' No, that's a misconception. In the big anthologies, there was more of that feeling [that] you got your submissions and you published them because it was really important to have everybody's voice heard. But when it came down to the individual books, like *Eating Artichokes*, it wasn't like we just slapped the thing together and printed it. There was some sort of selective process."

Indeed, not everything written by lesbians is printed today. Kim's chapbook of poems, *Eating Artichokes*, was the first work by an openly lesbian Asian to be published. Kim says that, while the work of such Asian lesbian writers as Merle Woo, Canyon Sam, and Barbara Noda has been included in anthologies, few Asian lesbians have had their work published in book form. "It's a real sobering statement when you think about that," Kim notes. "I didn't have to wait ten years to get my prose published; I was very fortunate that Alyson wanted my works of fiction. But there's also that Asian stereotype, that Asians are the last out of the closet. It's a hard thing to combat.

"I was extremely shy growing up—just dreaded speaking out in class," Kim recalls. "So it's been a struggle for me to be vocal—or even if somebody asks me to be on a panel, I would much rather defer to someone else. But I realize how important it is to be a part of ongoing verbalization of being an Asian lesbian.

"Merle Woo, a long time ago, said that she read everything that I'd ever written, and she said, 'You know, for the longest time, you were the only lesbian Asian that I knew; your [work] was the only [writing] that I ever read that was by anybody Asian.' And that shows you how important it is to at least try to get your [work] out there. Merle got hold of my [writing] through *Eating Artichokes,* through the publishing [of] the Women's Press Collective; if they hadn't printed that book, Merle wouldn't have had that contact.

"*I* know that there are *hundreds* of Asian lesbians," Kim points out. "And you can't get your [writing published outside] of the anthologies? That's ridiculous. That's shocking, that [publishers are] not interested enough. I don't know why it is, this big discrepancy; I don't know."

The shy kid who wrote a prize-winning baseball story has grown up to play an important role in lesbian culture and history. Carrying her manuscript of poems with her to a women's bookstore, Willyce Kim joined a movement that had given voice to lesbians and added to it the words of an Asian sister. Even Dancer and the Kid couldn't have come up with a greater adventure.

Works by Willyce Kim: *Dancer Dawkins and the California Kid* (Alyson Publications, 1985); *Dead Heat* (Alyson Publications, 1988); *Eating Artichokes* (Women's Press Collective, 1972)

21.

Lesléa Newman

Writing From the Heart

There was no question about what Lesléa
Newman was going to be when she grew up. "I've
been writing ever since I can remember," she recalls.
"I've always wanted to be a writer, since I was a
little girl, and I used to write poetry—really lousy
poetry!" Newman admits with a laugh.

"[When] I went to college, of course, people said,
'You can't be a writer; you have to be something
else.' So I designed a major of creative writing and
social services in the education department. I still

Interview conducted March 24, 1991.

was writing only poetry. Then I went to the Naropa Institute, in Boulder, Colorado, where I studied with people like Allen Ginsberg. And then, after a few years, I decided I had to go to graduate school, because that's what real writers do.

"So I went to Boston University for one semester, then dropped out—because I really couldn't stand it—and I had a year of being really depressed. Then I came out [as a lesbian], and felt much better! I started writing again, and I started writing fiction, which I had never written before."

Newman's newly acknowledged lesbianism, her renewal of interest in writing, and the growth of her work into new areas led to her successful career as an openly lesbian and highly prolific writer in an unusual variety of genres: novels, poetry, short stories, children's books. Newman has also worked as an anthology editor, and her own writing has been included in a number of anthologies.

Each genre in which she writes offers Newman different satisfactions. "A poem is wonderful because you can write it in one day," she notes with a laugh. "It gives you instant gratification.

"A novel is really wonderful because the hardest thing for me about writing is starting fresh with just a blank piece of paper in front of me after I've finished something. With a novel, you have something to go back to, an ongoing project for a year or longer. So that's really wonderful.

"And a short story is in between. Usually, for me, it takes about two weeks to write a short story, so I have something to do for a couple of weeks. And I like that, because it's like dropping in on someone for a short visit."

Newman says that she doesn't have a conscious plan as to what form a new work will take. "I never really decide ahead of time what I'm going to sit down and write; really, the form comes out of the content. I start with an image, or I start with a character, and I see where the writing takes me. The writing is my teacher. I try really hard not to put myself and my expectations on top of it. I try and really let *it* lead me."

Newman offers some examples. "I was not expecting to write my newest novel, *In Every Laugh A Tear.* I wrote a short story about a ninety-nine-year-old Jewish woman, and then it was really clear to me that I had too much to tell, and I really did have to write a novel. It's so terrifying to start a novel, so I wasn't really looking forward to it, and I really tried to avoid it! But then it became inevitable."

Similarly, Liza Goldberg, the wisecracking protagonist of Newman's novel *Good Enough to Eat,* "really revealed herself to *me.* And I was really glad that she had this wonderful sense of humor, or else it would have been much too painful to spend the amount of time I had to spend with her! So, her character and personality emerged as I did more writing about her."

While most writers need to hold other jobs to support their underpaid (or unpaid) creative work, Newman has managed to remain totally in the literary realm by teaching writing to earn a living. "When I first started doing my workshops, I worked part-time as a secretary," Newman explains. "And then, basically, I made the commitment [to write and teach writing] because I've never been happy doing anything else. There was not a choice; this had to succeed, because there was nothing left for me to do. As I got to a healthier place in myself spiritually and emotionally, I couldn't tolerate things that were no good for me—and one thing that was really not good for me was being a secretary.

"So I took a major leap. I came up with a name for my business, 'Write From the Heart.' Everything is aboveboard; I take taxes out, I treat it like a business. And if it's not going well, then it's up to me to create something that *will* go well. It's up to me to keep thinking of new ways to market what I know how to do."

While Newman is one of the rare writers whose livelihood is financially as well as spiritually profitable, she finds it "ironic that I'm making my living teaching writing" since "one of the reasons I dropped out of graduate school was because I had a teaching fellowship, and I was *terrified* of teaching! I just froze." But in 1985, after spending a few months at home writing a novel and living off an insurance settlement, Newman changed her mind. "I couldn't face going back to work for anybody else, so I decided to work for myself. I hung up posters and put ads in the newspaper, and got my first class together and started that way."

Not surprisingly, Newman's workshops reflect the variety of her own writings. "One ongoing workshop is called 'Write From the Heart'; that's the basic workshop for women who want to write, but are scared to try, or who had a bad experience in school, or who don't really feel they have anything important to say," Newman explains. "Then I have 'Poems From the Heart,' which focuses on poetry; 'A

Novel Idea,' which is for women who are working on novels; and 'What Are You Eating/What's Eating You,' which is a writing workshop focusing on body image and eating patterns.

"Then, every month, I do a different one-day workshop. For example, in May, I do one called 'We Are All Daughters,' which is writing exercises focused on the mother/daughter relationship. I do one for Jewish women called 'Generating Memories/Remembering Generations,' where we write in the voices of our maternal ancestors. And I do one called 'Luscious Letters,' which is lesbian love poetry; I usually do that right before Valentine's Day."

While Newman acknowledges that "at least half my students are not interested in being professional writers—they just like to write, or want to write because it makes them feel better," she points out that "I treat them all as professional writers, because I feel like that's what they're [paying for], and that they want that knowledge from me."

Newman explains, "I don't think writing is self-expression as much as it's communication. I tell my students, 'If you just want to express yourself, you don't need to pay me to teach you how to do that. If you want to communicate, that's different.'

"So there's a good part of learning how to write dialogue; how to describe a character; how to show, not tell. In every class, we do at least two spontaneous twenty-minute writing exercises, where I will suggest an idea that might sound off-the-wall, but will just sort of juggle [the students'] brains in a way that wouldn't [happen] if they were at home just looking at a blank piece of paper, thinking 'What do I do now?' "

Is there ever a conflict between what Newman wants to teach her students and what they want to learn? "I think the conflict comes when somebody doesn't want to get feedback on their writing," Newman replies. "You know, a lot of people want to be writers but they don't want to write. They don't want to work as hard as you have to work. They just want to write it once; they don't want to rewrite it. They want to be finished with it and go write something else and get pats on the head. And I won't do that. As I said, if you really want that, you don't need to take a class; you could just write something and show it to your friends and they'll tell you how wonderful you are.

"I'm not a real *harsh* critic. I never rip someone's writing to shreds, or use words like 'bad,' 'awful,' 'stupid.' I really try to take what they have written and what they've said, and teach them how to say it better and more effectively. I definitely encourage, rather than discourage. But, as a good teacher, I feel that it's important for me to challenge my students, and for them to learn how to challenge themselves."

Newman's methods have worked; her students have had work published in anthologies and literary magazines, and some have enrolled in master of fine arts programs. And, conversely, Newman says of her writing workshops, "Over the years, I've really learned a lot about teaching, and about writing—I feel like my students are also my teachers."

It was Newman's willingness to listen to the ideas of others that led to her writing her first children's book, *Heather Has Two Mommies*, which was written for the daughter of a friend. The book, about the young daughter of lesbian mothers, started its life as a self-published venture. "I rooked a friend into doing it with me, because she had a desktop publishing business," Newman admits. "I have a pretty substantial mailing list from readings and workshops I've done around the country. So we sent out a fundraising letter [that said] what the book was about, and [saying that] if anybody wanted to give us a donation of ten dollars or more, they would get this book in about a year's time. We raised about four thousand dollars that way."

After Newman printed the book and sold half of the press run, she received a letter from Sasha Alyson, founder of the gay/lesbian press Alyson Publications, who had started a children's book imprint called Alyson Wonderland. "Sasha wrote to us and told us about [Alyson Wonderland]," Newman relates. "He said, 'I've never heard of you; are you just a one-book press? Because if you are, I know [that] a lot of times it's more work than it's worth; [and] if at any time your book is going to go out of print, please contact me.' I called him up the day I got the letter and said, 'Sasha, *please!* I want my living room back!' So we made a deal, and we were in business. It's definitely a happily-ever-after story; it's what every self-published author would want."

Newman's newfound fame as a children's book author has had its drawbacks, however. She recalls, "*Heather* was written up in *Newsweek*. It really got quite amazing publicity, which is wonderful, and at the same time, a lot of people only know me as the writer of *Heather Has Two Mommies*, and that's really frustrating for me, because I take my fiction writing and my poetry for adults *very* seriously!"

A striking attribute of Newman's writing for

adults is the strong Jewish voice of her characters. Why did she decide to give her protagonists two "outsider" identities: as lesbian *and* Jewish? "I deliberately wrote [the book] *A Letter to Harvey Milk* to answer the questions I had about 'What does it mean to be a Jewish lesbian' and 'What does it mean to be a lesbian Jew,'" Newman responds. "I think of myself as one or the other depending on what day it is and how I feel.

"So I really wrote that book because I hadn't read a book like that, and I wanted to answer those questions for myself. For me—and I've heard this from a lot of other lesbians—when I came out as a lesbian, I came out as a Jew. I was never in the closet [about] being a Jew, but I became much stronger in that identity when I came out [as a lesbian]. I think it's because when you're a lesbian, it's really clear you're an outsider, so you might as well be who you fully are. So when I came out as a lesbian, I really felt like I could be fully myself, and it was to my extreme delight that being a Jew was such a big part of that."

A published writer, a teacher of writing, a woman at peace with herself: by most criteria, Lesléa Newman is a success. What is success to her? "I suppose the fact that my work is in print is a success," she reflects. "I think for me, when the writing is going well, that's as much of a success as I care about, and I don't really care so much about whether it gets published or not. Which might sound odd, because I do publish a lot, and I work at that.

"But when I wrote my first novel, I had a party when I finished the novel, not when I got the contract and not when the book came out. Because for me, the personal success of sustaining a novel was the most important thing." But Newman admits with a laugh, "That's one side of me talking! The other side of me says, 'A Pulitzer Prize—then I would feel successful!' "

But she continues, "You know, it's always enough and it's never enough. I keep striving to improve myself and improve my writing, explore different forms, explore different content. I don't think that I would feel more successful, for example, if a mainstream house published me. That's really not my measure of success. I think the fact that I can orchestrate my life so that I have time to write every day is an enormous measure of success, and that's really what's the most important thing to me."

Works by Lesléa Newman: *Good Enough to Eat* (Firebrand Books, 1986; Sheba Feminist Publishers [London], 1986); *In Every Laugh A Tear* (New Victoria Publishers, 1992); *A Letter to Harvey Milk* (Firebrand Books, 1988); *Secrets* (New Victoria Publishers, 1990); *Just Looking for My Shoes* (Back Door Press, 1980); *Love Me Like You Mean It* (HerBooks, 1987); *Sweet Dark Places* (HerBooks, 1991); *SomeBody to Love: A Guide to Loving the Body You Have* (Third Side Press, 1991); *Bubbe Meisehs by Shayneh Maidelehs: An Anthology of Poetry by Jewish Granddaughters About Our Grandmothers* (HerBooks, 1989); *Eating Our Hearts Out: Women and Food* (Crossing Press, 1993); *Heather Has Two Mommies* (In Other Words Publishing, 1989; reprinted by Alyson Wonderland,

1990); *Gloria Goes to Gay Pride* (Alyson Wonderland, 1991); *Belinda's Bouquet* (Alyson Wonderland, 1991); *Saturday Is Pattyday* (New Victoria Publishers and Women's Educational Press [Toronto], 1993)

22.

Terri de la Peña

"I Wrote This Book
Because I Wanted to Read It"

"I was a very late bloomer with *everything,*" Terri
de la Peña admits with a laugh. "I played with dolls
until I was twelve, until I started realizing that
nobody else my age was still playing with them, and
I started feeling really *strange.*

"That was a real big part of my life, this whole
fantasy world thing, so somehow or other—and I'm
not sure *exactly* how—I started writing. It became a
substitute so I could still have my characters, but I

Interview conducted May 2, 1992.

was writing about them, instead of actually playing with them like I used to."

De la Peña adds, "I'm the middle child in the family—two older, two younger—and I was always the real quiet one [who] didn't do much, or [the one who the family] always thought was in this dream world; you know, 'Terri's the dreamer.' Their attitude [was] that I was never going to amount to anything. And so now, everybody's kind of shocked. Really, they don't quite know what to make of it. Because [my family] has known that I've been doing this [writing] for *years*; I just wasn't published, and so it was just, 'Oh, yeah, Terri writes.'"

What "shocked" de la Peña's family was the publication of her first novel, *Margins,* in 1992. The story of a young Chicana lesbian, Veronica Melendez, and her efforts to recover from the death of her lover, form a new relationship, come out to her family, and pursue her dream of writing, *Margins* took ten years from first draft to publication, as de la Peña struggled with her own process of coming out as a lesbian.

"I really had started *Margins* in 1982, and I had put it aside because I couldn't go any further until I came out," de la Peña acknowledges. "*Margins* was in the closet, literally. I couldn't do it, because I wasn't out! Just couldn't write those things, because I hadn't lived them. But once I took [the manuscript] out again and started to get going, it was five years later, and I had already been through [a lot of those] experiences."

It was de la Peña's writing that helped her to come to terms with her lesbianism. "I think I realized when the writing started getting more lesbian that it was bound to happen, that one was going to lead to the other," she states. One of her stories, "A Saturday in August," was about "a Chicana feminist who met a Chicana lesbian. And at that point [the story was written in 1983], I was the Chicana feminist; I wasn't the lesbian yet. I hadn't come out; I was right on the verge of coming out. And I think that's the story that did it."

"A Saturday in August" had an effect on de la Peña's life as a writer, as well. It was the story she had submitted to qualify as a member of a local Latina writers group, and it was the story that another member of the group encouraged her to enter in the Chicano literary competition sponsored by the department of Spanish and Portuguese of the University of California (UC) at Irvine.

"She said, 'If you don't enter this contest, I'm going to send your manuscript in *for* you!'" de la Peña recounts with a laugh. "I was really tired of her bugging me about this, so finally I said, 'Okay, I'll do it.' And so I was goaded into it; I didn't really think I had a chance. And I won third prize, out of a hundred competitors."

However, as de la Peña recalls, "When I won the contest, I wasn't writing anything. I was at a job where I just didn't have any free time. I used to work late, and I was going to school at night—I had no time to write fiction. And when I won the contest, it was just shocking, because I had written that story in 1983, and I won in 1986, so there was that period in there where I wasn't writing—but I won a contest!"

But de la Peña soon returned to writing, thanks to the support and encouragement of Chicana writer

Helena Maria Viramontes, one of the judges of the UC Irvine contest. "Helena stayed in touch with me, and she would call me every once in a while and say, 'Well, what are you working on now?'" de la Peña recalls. "And I said, 'I'm not working on anything.' Helena said, 'What's the matter with you?!' I said, 'I don't have time!' And Helena said, 'Well, you won this [contest]—it's supposed to open doors.' And so she started me thinking that, okay, since I won this, and since I won with a Chicana lesbian character in the story, maybe I really *should* do something with this [writing], and go public."

One way in which de la Peña "went public" was to write book reviews for the Los Angeles–based *Lesbian News*. In the process, de la Peña recalls, "I started reading a lot of lesbian novels, and came to the realization that *I* could do it." And so she began working on *Margins* again.

By this time (the late 1980s), de la Peña had reassurance that an audience existed for novels and stories about Chicanas. But earlier in the decade, she had been feeling more isolated as a Chicana writer, until she discovered the work of other Chicana feminists. "[When I read] *This Bridge Called My Back* [the anthology edited by Cherríe Moraga and Gloria Anzaldúa], that got me very excited," de la Peña remembers. "I still wasn't quite out yet—I was thinking about coming out, but I wasn't quite out—and I was doing these stories about Chicana feminists. And [when I read *Bridge*], that's when I started really getting more enthused about [my writing]; I just didn't know where to send the stories! I was writing them, but I didn't know where they would go—so they didn't go anywhere!" de la Peña laughs.

But *Margins* went (successfully) to Seal Press, a feminist press in Seattle, Washington. When de la Peña told other Chicana writers of her acquaintance that she had submitted her manuscript to Seal, "They said, 'Good.' Everybody's attitude was 'Yes, go with the women.' Because there's so much sexism in the Chicano community. [Some Chicanos] tend not to take us [women] seriously, and if we're lesbians, well, forget it!

"When I get a call for submissions [to lesbian/feminist anthologies], it usually says, 'We especially encourage work by women of color,'" de la Peña points out. "I mean, they're *looking* for us. So, especially after doing those book reviews, I figured, okay, I *see* what [little is] out there, as far as fiction goes. And that's what I want to write. And so I figured, I'm going to have a good chance. And I did!"

De la Peña's artistic ambition is much influenced by her desire to add another Chicana voice to the spectrum of contemporary literature. "That has a lot to do with it," de la Peña acknowledges. "And not specifically Chicana lesbian, actually, but Chicana, because there are so few of us doing this [writing] who are getting published. I feel like there's a need for Chicana/Chicano stories, period, and if I can throw the lesbian angle in, too, fine, but I don't necessarily have to, because the need for the stories is so great. *Especially* now that I'm speaking to Chicano studies classes, I really see it—I mean, [the students] are just *hungry* for it.

"When I was younger, I used to only write about

white people," de la Peña admits. "I had never read anything about Chicanos, so how could I write that, even though it was my experience! I didn't start writing about Chicanos and Chicanas until around 1980. And that was my intention [then], to be a Chicana writer.

"Right after that, I came out, so then the focus started changing a little bit," de la Peña continues. "[My] audience is now wider; it's Chicana/Chicano and it's gay/lesbian and it's feminist. So I feel real lucky that way, that I've been able to reach all three."

De la Peña's pride in her identity as a Chicana writer is evident in her work. The characters in *Margins* speak Spanish frequently, with de la Peña's usage of her mother's native language reflecting the manner in which it typically is spoken in Mexican American communities.

"It's very true in the Chicano community: you have people who don't speak any Spanish at all, you have people who don't speak any English at all, and you have people who speak both," de la Peña explains. "And then you have people like me, who understand Spanish but feel more confident speaking English. So I was trying to show that in *Margins,* too."

Margins draws on its author's life for its narrative framework in ways other than use of language. But de la Peña notes that the book "is *not* really autobiographical, because Veronica's much smarter than I was at that age; I didn't come out until I was thirty-six, and she's twenty-two. So a lot of it is wishful thinking; I wish I were like Veronica!" she declares with a laugh.

But other differences between the author and her protagonist are very deliberate. "I don't have a college education," de la Peña says, "but I wanted to have Veronica be in college. I felt this was important as a statement that *not* all Chicanas are dropouts; some of us *do* go to college, some of us *do* have opportunities.

"Also, [Veronica's family is] middle class, emerging from the working class. I thought it was really important to write about [Chicano] people who were not in the barrio. Because we're so stereotyped; I never grew up in a barrio, I grew up in Santa Monica [California], in a beach town, and I felt like I could never find anybody like me in fiction."

De la Peña is determined to correct this imbalance. After *Margins'* publication, she compiled a collection of short stories titled *Territories.* "It has stories written between 1980 and 1992," de la Peña explains. "Some have lesbian characters, some do not. It's a very Chicana/Chicano group of stories; it has male characters, too."

And de la Peña's future projects also will be very much about "people like her": her next novel, and also what she calls "growing-up stories, from childhood up to adolescence. I want to write about people that I grew up with, but [whom I will] fictionalize. I want to bring [the characters] up to adolescence, and just stop there. It would be like a preview of *Margins,* although it won't be [about] Veronica, it will be somebody else, probably the sisters in [my story] 'Once a Friend.'

"There's just very little out there like that, Chicana [writing]," de la Peña declares. "I don't know if [these projects] would really be considered

lesbian; I don't know *what* [they] would be considered. I'm trying to get *Margins* [taught] in classes;
my short stories already have been included in
readings for Chicana feminism classes and in a
sociology course on contemporary Chicano issues.

"I'm the first Chicana that Seal Press has
published, and I really want [everyone] to know that
there's a need for this [kind of writing]," de la Peña
adds. "I wrote [*Margins*] because I wanted to read it,
because I couldn't find anything like it."

Not that de la Peña, an avid reader, wasn't
looking. Lesbian/feminist literature had a profound
effect on her life long before she started writing it
herself. It was reading about lesbianism that helped
de la Peña to acknowledge her own identity. And in
Margins, when Veronica wants to explain to her
lover Siena (whose relationship with Veronica is her
first sexual experience with a woman) about the
lesbian community, she takes Siena to the local
women's bookstore and shows her the lesbian books.

In fact, it is lesbian/feminist literature, rather
than gay literature as a whole, from which de la
Peña currently derives her influences and inspiration.
"The first gay male novel I read was *City of Night,*
by John Rechy," de la Peña recalls, adding with a
laugh, "I really liked it! At the time [sometime in
the 1970s], I was working on this [unpublished]
novel about Chicano brothers, and so, to read
Rechy's work was, to me, very validating, because he
was writing about Chicanos, too. And then, one of
the reasons why I stopped working on [my novel]
was because I thought, [Rechy] *is* a gay male
Chicano, and he does it so well that I feel really

stupid doing this! And why am I writing about men, anyway?

"I think there's just a tremendous difference between men and women," de la Peña continues, "and our way of thinking is so different that I tend not to read [gay male literature]. I just don't like being lumped together with men. I think we're real different, we're separate. And I think there *is* some literature that crosses over, but *I* just want to be considered a Chicana lesbian writer, not really a gay writer. Although one review in Los Angeles has already called me a 'queer' writer, and [that] really bothered me. I don't like that word!" de la Peña asserts.

But despite her reluctance to accept the inevitable labels that critics and readers bestow on writers, de la Peña is enjoying the life of a published, and public, novelist—*most* of the time. "I still feel pretty private," she remarks. "I'm known in the lesbian community and in the Chicana community, [but] not really that much. I still don't think it's overwhelming; I can deal with it. I still give people my [home] phone number and my work number," she adds with a laugh.

"The only thing that's a little scary is if I'm walking down the street and somebody recognizes me, and I don't know who *they* are," de la Peña admits. "*That* is a little jolting, because it makes me more self-conscious than I already am. I'm not paranoid about it, but it makes me more aware that people might be watching me and I don't realize they are."

Judging by the enthusiastic reception that

Margins has been receiving in the Chicana/Chicano and lesbian communities, though, Terri de la Peña will have to become accustomed to being noticed by admirers. This "late bloomer" is quickly, and successfully, making up for lost time.

Works by Terri de la Peña: *Margins* (Seal Press, 1992); *Territories* (forthcoming from the Department of Spanish and Portuguese, University of California Irvine)

Resource List

Aché
P.O. Box 6071
Albany, CA 94706
(510) 849-2819

Deneuve
2336 Market Street, #15
San Francisco, CA 94114
(415) 863-6538

Feminist Bookstore News
P.O. Box 882554
San Francisco, CA 94188
(415) 626-1556

HOT WIRE: The Journal of Women's Music and Culture
5210 North Wayne
Chicago, IL 60640
(312) 769-9009

Kitchen Table: Women of Color Press
P.O. Box 908
Latham, NY 12110
(518) 434-2057

Lesbian Herstory Archives
P.O. Box 1258
New York, NY 10116
(718) 768-DYKE (3953)

The Naiad Press, Inc.
P.O. Box 10543
Tallahassee, FL 32302
(904) 539-5965

WIM (Women in the Moon) Publications
10203 Parkwood Drive, #7
Cupertino, CA 95014-1466
(408) 253-3329

Write From the Heart (Lesléa Newman)
P.O. Box 815
Northampton, MA 01061
(413) 584-3865

A few of the publications of
THE NAIAD PRESS, INC.
P.O. Box 10543 • Tallahassee, Florida 32302
Phone (904) 539-5965
Mail orders welcome. Please include 15% postage.

HAPPY ENDINGS by Kate Brandt. 272 pp. Intimate conversations
with Lesbian authors. ISBN 1-56280-050-7 $10.95

THE SPY IN QUESTION by Amanda Kyle Williams. 256 pp. 4th
spy novel featuring Lesbian agent Madison McGuire.
ISBN 1-56280-037-X 9.95

SAVING GRACE by Jennifer Fulton. 240 pp. Adventure and
romantic entanglement. ISBN 1-56280-051-5 9.95

THE YEAR SEVEN by Molleen Zanger. 208 pp. Women surviving
in a new world. ISBN 1-56280-034-5 9.95

CURIOUS WINE by Katherine V. Forrest. 176 pp. Tenth
Anniversary Edition. The most popular contemporary Lesbian
love story. ISBN 1-56280-053-1 9.95

CHAUTAUQUA by Catherine Ennis. 192 pp. Exciting, romantic
adventure. ISBN 1-56280-032-9 9.95

A PROPER BURIAL by Pat Welch. 192 pp. Third in the Helen
Black mystery series. ISBN 1-56280-033-7 9.95

SILVERLAKE HEAT: A Novel of Suspense by Carol Schmidt.
240 pp. Rhonda is as hot as Laney's dreams. ISBN 1-56280-031-0 9.95

LOVE, ZENA BETH by Diane Salvatore. 224 pp. The most talked
about lesbian novel of the nineties! ISBN 1-56280-030-2 9.95

A DOORYARD FULL OF FLOWERS by Isabel Miller. 160 pp.
Stories incl. 2 sequels to *Patience and Sarah.* ISBN 1-56280-029-9 9.95

MURDER BY TRADITION by Katherine V. Forrest. 288 pp. A
Kate Delafield Mystery. 4th in a series. ISBN 1-56280-002-7 9.95

THE EROTIC NAIAD edited by Katherine V. Forrest & Barbara Grier.
224 pp. Love stories by Naiad Press authors. ISBN 1-56280-026-4 12.95

DEAD CERTAIN by Claire McNab. 224 pp. 5th Det. Insp. Carol
Ashton mystery. ISBN 1-56280-027-2 9.95

CRAZY FOR LOVING by Jaye Maiman. 320 pp. 2nd Robin
Miller mystery. ISBN 1-56280-025-6 9.95

STONEHURST by Barbara Johnson. 176 pp. Passionate regency
romance. ISBN 1-56280-024-8 9.95

INTRODUCING AMANDA VALENTINE by Rose Beecham.
256 pp. An Amanda Valentine Mystery — 1st in a series.
ISBN 1-56280-021-3   9.95

UNCERTAIN COMPANIONS by Robbi Sommers. 204 pp.
Steamy, erotic novel.   ISBN 1-56280-017-5   9.95

A TIGER'S HEART by Lauren W. Douglas. 240 pp. Fourth Caitlin
Reece Mystery.   ISBN 1-56280-018-3   9.95

PAPERBACK ROMANCE by Karin Kallmaker. 256 pp. A
delicious romance.   ISBN 1-56280-019-1   9.95

MORTON RIVER VALLEY by Lee Lynch. 304 pp. Lee Lynch at
her best!   ISBN 1-56280-016-7   9.95

THE LAVENDER HOUSE MURDER by Nikki Baker. 224 pp. A
Virginia Kelly Mystery. Second in a series.   ISBN 1-56280-012-4   9.95

PASSION BAY by Jennifer Fulton. 224 pp. Passionate romance,
virgin beaches, tropical skies.   ISBN 1-56280-028-0   9.95

STICKS AND STONES by Jackie Calhoun. 208 pp. Contemporary
lesbian lives and loves.   ISBN 1-56280-020-5   9.95

DELIA IRONFOOT by Jeane Harris. 192 pp. Adventure for Delia
and Beth in the Utah mountains.   ISBN 1-56280-014-0   9.95

UNDER THE SOUTHERN CROSS by Claire McNab. 192 pp.
Romantic nights Down Under.   ISBN 1-56280-011-6   9.95

RIVERFINGER WOMEN by Elana Nachman/Dykewomon.
208 pp. Classic Lesbian/feminist novel.   ISBN 1-56280-013-2   8.95

A CERTAIN DISCONTENT by Cleve Boutell. 240 pp. A unique
coterie of women.   ISBN 1-56280-009-4   9.95

GRASSY FLATS by Penny Hayes. 256 pp. Lesbian romance in
the '30s.   ISBN 1-56280-010-8   9.95

A SINGULAR SPY by Amanda K. Williams. 192 pp. 3rd spy novel
featuring Lesbian agent Madison McGuire.   ISBN 1-56280-008-6   8.95

THE END OF APRIL by Penny Sumner. 240 pp. A Victoria Cross
Mystery. First in a series.   ISBN 1-56280-007-8   8.95

A FLIGHT OF ANGELS by Sarah Aldridge. 240 pp. Romance set at
the National Gallery of Art   ISBN 1-56280-001-9   9.95

HOUSTON TOWN by Deborah Powell. 208 pp. A Hollis Carpenter
mystery. Second in a series.   ISBN 1-56280-006-X   8.95

KISS AND TELL by Robbi Sommers. 192 pp. Scorching stories by
the author of *Pleasures*.   ISBN 1-56280-005-1   9.95

STILL WATERS by Pat Welch. 208 pp. Second in the Helen
Black mystery series.   ISBN 0-941483-97-5   9.95

MURDER IS GERMANE by Karen Saum. 224 pp. The 2nd
Brigid Donovan mystery.   ISBN 0-941483-98-3   8.95

TO LOVE AGAIN by Evelyn Kennedy. 208 pp. Wildly
romantic love story.   ISBN 0-941483-85-1   9.95

IN THE GAME by Nikki Baker. 192 pp. A Virginia Kelly
mystery. First in a series.   ISBN 01-56280-004-3 9.95

AVALON by Mary Jane Jones. 256 pp. A Lesbian Arthurian
romance.   ISBN 0-941483-96-7   9.95

STRANDED by Camarin Grae. 320 pp. Entertaining, riveting
adventure.   ISBN 0-941483-99-1   9.95

THE DAUGHTERS OF ARTEMIS by Lauren Wright Douglas.
240 pp. Third Caitlin Reece mystery.   ISBN 0-941483-95-9   9.95

CLEARWATER by Catherine Ennis. 176 pp. Romantic secrets
of a small Louisiana town.   ISBN 0-941483-65-7   8.95

THE HALLELUJAH MURDERS by Dorothy Tell. 176 pp.
Second Poppy Dillworth mystery.   ISBN 0-941483-88-6   8.95

ZETA BASE by Judith Alguire. 208 pp. Lesbian triangle
on a future Earth.   ISBN 0-941483-94-0   9.95

SECOND CHANCE by Jackie Calhoun. 256 pp. Contemporary
Lesbian lives and loves.   ISBN 0-941483-93-2   9.95

BENEDICTION by Diane Salvatore. 272 pp. Striking,
contemporary romantic novel.   ISBN 0-941483-90-8   9.95

CALLING RAIN by Karen Marie Christa Minns. 240 pp.
Spellbinding, erotic love story   ISBN 0-941483-87-8   9.95

BLACK IRIS by Jeane Harris. 192 pp. Caroline's hidden past . . .
                                        ISBN 0-941483-68-1   8.95

TOUCHWOOD by Karin Kallmaker. 240 pp. Loving, May/
December romance.   ISBN 0-941483-76-2   9.95

BAYOU CITY SECRETS by Deborah Powell. 224 pp. A Hollis
Carpenter mystery. First in a series.   ISBN 0-941483-91-6   9.95

COP OUT by Claire McNab. 208 pp. 4th Det. Insp. Carol Ashton
mystery.   ISBN 0-941483-84-3   9.95

LODESTAR by Phyllis Horn. 224 pp. Romantic, fast-moving
adventure.   ISBN 0-941483-83-5   8.95

THE BEVERLY MALIBU by Katherine V. Forrest. 288 pp. A
Kate Delafield Mystery. 3rd in a series. ISBN 0-941483-48-7   9.95

THAT OLD STUDEBAKER by Lee Lynch. 272 pp. Andy's affair
with Regina and her attachment to her beloved car.
                                        ISBN 0-941483-82-7   9.95

PASSION'S LEGACY by Lori Paige. 224 pp. Sarah is swept into
the arms of Augusta Pym in this delightful historical romance.
                                        ISBN 0-941483-81-9   8.95

THE PROVIDENCE FILE by Amanda Kyle Williams. 256 pp.
Second espionage thriller featuring lesbian agent Madison McGuire
ISBN 0-941483-92-4   8.95

I LEFT MY HEART by Jaye Maiman. 320 pp. A Robin Miller
Mystery. First in a series.   ISBN 0-941483-72-X   9.95

THE PRICE OF SALT by Patricia Highsmith (writing as Claire
Morgan). 288 pp. Classic lesbian novel, first issued in 1952 . . .
acknowledged by its author under her own, very famous, name.
ISBN 1-56280-003-5   9.95

SIDE BY SIDE by Isabel Miller. 256 pp. From beloved author of
Patience and Sarah.   ISBN 0-941483-77-0   9.95

SOUTHBOUND by Sheila Ortiz Taylor. 240 pp. Hilarious sequel
to *Faultline.*   ISBN 0-941483-78-9   8.95

STAYING POWER: LONG TERM LESBIAN COUPLES
by Susan E. Johnson. 352 pp. Joys of coupledom.
ISBN 0-941-483-75-4   12.95

SLICK by Camarin Grae. 304 pp. Exotic, erotic adventure.
ISBN 0-941483-74-6   9.95

NINTH LIFE by Lauren Wright Douglas. 256 pp. A Caitlin
Reece mystery. 2nd in a series.   ISBN 0-941483-50-9   8.95

PLAYERS by Robbi Sommers. 192 pp. Sizzling, erotic novel.
ISBN 0-941483-73-8   9.95

MURDER AT RED ROOK RANCH by Dorothy Tell. 224 pp.
First Poppy Dillworth adventure.   ISBN 0-941483-80-0   8.95

LESBIAN SURVIVAL MANUAL by Rhonda Dicksion.
112 pp. Cartoons!   ISBN 0-941483-71-1   8.95

A ROOM FULL OF WOMEN by Elisabeth Nonas. 256 pp.
Contemporary Lesbian lives.   ISBN 0-941483-69-X   9.95

MURDER IS RELATIVE by Karen Saum. 256 pp. The first
Brigid Donovan mystery.   ISBN 0-941483-70-3   8.95

PRIORITIES by Lynda Lyons 288 pp. Science fiction with
a twist.   ISBN 0-941483-66-5   8.95

THEME FOR DIVERSE INSTRUMENTS by Jane Rule. 208
pp. Powerful romantic lesbian stories.   ISBN 0-941483-63-0   8.95

LESBIAN QUERIES by Hertz & Ertman. 112 pp. The questions
you were too embarrassed to ask.   ISBN 0-941483-67-3   8.95

CLUB 12 by Amanda Kyle Williams. 288 pp. Espionage thriller
featuring a lesbian agent!   ISBN 0-941483-64-9   8.95

DEATH DOWN UNDER by Claire McNab. 240 pp. 3rd Det.
Insp. Carol Ashton mystery.   ISBN 0-941483-39-8   9.95

MONTANA FEATHERS by Penny Hayes. 256 pp. Vivian and
Elizabeth find love in frontier Montana.   ISBN 0-941483-61-4   8.95

CHESAPEAKE PROJECT by Phyllis Horn. 304 pp. Jessie & Meredith in perilous adventure. ISBN 0-941483-58-4   8.95

LIFESTYLES by Jackie Calhoun. 224 pp. Contemporary Lesbian lives and loves. ISBN 0-941483-57-6   9.95

VIRAGO by Karen Marie Christa Minns. 208 pp. Darsen has chosen Ginny. ISBN 0-941483-56-8   8.95

WILDERNESS TREK by Dorothy Tell. 192 pp. Six women on vacation learning "new" skills. ISBN 0-941483-60-6   8.95

MURDER BY THE BOOK by Pat Welch. 256 pp. A Helen Black Mystery. First in a series. ISBN 0-941483-59-2   9.95

BERRIGAN by Vicki P. McConnell. 176 pp. Youthful Lesbian — romantic, idealistic Berrigan. ISBN 0-941483-55-X   8.95

LESBIANS IN GERMANY by Lillian Faderman & B. Eriksson. 128 pp. Fiction, poetry, essays. ISBN 0-941483-62-2   8.95

THERE'S SOMETHING I'VE BEEN MEANING TO TELL YOU Ed. by Loralee MacPike. 288 pp. Gay men and lesbians coming out to their children. ISBN 0-941483-44-4   9.95

LIFTING BELLY by Gertrude Stein. Ed. by Rebecca Mark. 104 pp. Erotic poetry. ISBN 0-941483-51-7   8.95

ROSE PENSKI by Roz Perry. 192 pp. Adult lovers in a long-term relationship. ISBN 0-941483-37-1   8.95

AFTER THE FIRE by Jane Rule. 256 pp. Warm, human novel by this incomparable author. ISBN 0-941483-45-2   8.95

SUE SLATE, PRIVATE EYE by Lee Lynch. 176 pp. The gay folk of Peacock Alley are all cats. ISBN 0-941483-52-5   8.95

CHRIS by Randy Salem. 224 pp. Golden oldie. Handsome Chris and her adventures. ISBN 0-941483-42-8   8.95

THREE WOMEN by March Hastings. 232 pp. Golden oldie. A triangle among wealthy sophisticates. ISBN 0-941483-43-6   8.95

RICE AND BEANS by Valeria Taylor. 232 pp. Love and romance on poverty row. ISBN 0-941483-41-X   8.95

PLEASURES by Robbi Sommers. 204 pp. Unprecedented eroticism. ISBN 0-941483-49-5   8.95

EDGEWISE by Camarin Grae. 372 pp. Spellbinding adventure. ISBN 0-941483-19-3   9.95

FATAL REUNION by Claire McNab. 224 pp. 2nd Det. Inspec. Carol Ashton mystery. ISBN 0-941483-40-1   8.95

KEEP TO ME STRANGER by Sarah Aldridge. 372 pp. Romance set in a department store dynasty. ISBN 0-941483-38-X   9.95

HEARTSCAPE by Sue Gambill. 204 pp. American lesbian in Portugal. ISBN 0-941483-33-9   8.95

IN THE BLOOD by Lauren Wright Douglas. 252 pp. Lesbian
science fiction adventure fantasy   ISBN 0-941483-22-3   8.95

THE BEE'S KISS by Shirley Verel. 216 pp. Delicate, delicious
romance.   ISBN 0-941483-36-3   8.95

RAGING MOTHER MOUNTAIN by Pat Emmerson. 264 pp.
Furosa Firechild's adventures in Wonderland.   ISBN 0-941483-35-5   8.95

IN EVERY PORT by Karin Kallmaker. 228 pp. Jessica's sexy,
adventuresome travels.   ISBN 0-941483-37-7   9.95

OF LOVE AND GLORY by Evelyn Kennedy. 192 pp. Exciting
WWII romance.   ISBN 0-941483-32-0   8.95

CLICKING STONES by Nancy Tyler Glenn. 288 pp. Love
transcending time.   ISBN 0-941483-31-2   9.95

SURVIVING SISTERS by Gail Pass. 252 pp. Powerful love
story.   ISBN 0-941483-16-9   8.95

SOUTH OF THE LINE by Catherine Ennis. 216 pp. Civil War
adventure.   ISBN 0-941483-29-0   8.95

WOMAN PLUS WOMAN by Dolores Klaich. 300 pp. Supurb
Lesbian overview.   ISBN 0-941483-28-2   9.95

SLOW DANCING AT MISS POLLY'S by Sheila Ortiz Taylor.
96 pp. Lesbian Poetry   ISBN 0-941483-30-4   7.95

DOUBLE DAUGHTER by Vicki P. McConnell. 216 pp. A Nyla
Wade Mystery, third in the series.   ISBN 0-941483-26-6   8.95

HEAVY GILT by Delores Klaich. 192 pp. Lesbian detective/
disappearing homophobes/upper class gay society.
   ISBN 0-941483-25-8   8.95

THE FINER GRAIN by Denise Ohio. 216 pp. Brilliant young
college lesbian novel.   ISBN 0-941483-11-8   8.95

THE AMAZON TRAIL by Lee Lynch. 216 pp. Life, travel & lore
of famous lesbian author.   ISBN 0-941483-27-4   8.95

HIGH CONTRAST by Jessie Lattimore. 264 pp. Women of the
Crystal Palace.   ISBN 0-941483-17-7   8.95

OCTOBER OBSESSION by Meredith More. Josie's rich, secret
Lesbian life.   ISBN 0-941483-18-5   8.95

LESBIAN CROSSROADS by Ruth Baetz. 276 pp. Contemporary
Lesbian lives.   ISBN 0-941483-21-5   9.95

BEFORE STONEWALL: THE MAKING OF A GAY AND
LESBIAN COMMUNITY by Andrea Weiss & Greta Schiller.
96 pp., 25 illus.   ISBN 0-941483-20-7   7.95

WE WALK THE BACK OF THE TIGER by Patricia A. Murphy.
192 pp. Romantic Lesbian novel/beginning women's movement.
   ISBN 0-941483-13-4   8.95

SUNDAY'S CHILD by Joyce Bright. 216 pp. Lesbian athletics, at
last the novel about sports.   ISBN 0-941483-12-6   8.95

OSTEN'S BAY by Zenobia N. Vole. 204 pp. Sizzling adventure
romance set on Bonaire.   ISBN 0-941483-15-0   8.95

LESSONS IN MURDER by Claire McNab. 216 pp. 1st Det. Inspec.
Carol Ashton mystery — erotic tension!.   ISBN 0-941483-14-2   8.95

YELLOWTHROAT by Penny Hayes. 240 pp. Margarita, bandit,
kidnaps Julia.   ISBN 0-941483-10-X   8.95

SAPPHISTRY: THE BOOK OF LESBIAN SEXUALITY by
Pat Califia. 3d edition, revised. 208 pp.   ISBN 0-941483-24-X   10.95

CHERISHED LOVE by Evelyn Kennedy. 192 pp. Erotic
Lesbian love story.   ISBN 0-941483-08-8   9.95

LAST SEPTEMBER by Helen R. Hull. 208 pp. Six stories & a
glorious novella.   ISBN 0-941483-09-6   8.95

THE SECRET IN THE BIRD by Camarin Grae. 312 pp. Striking,
psychological suspense novel.   ISBN 0-941483-05-3   8.95

TO THE LIGHTNING by Catherine Ennis. 208 pp. Romantic
Lesbian 'Robinson Crusoe' adventure.   ISBN 0-941483-06-1   8.95

THE OTHER SIDE OF VENUS by Shirley Verel. 224 pp.
Luminous, romantic love story.   ISBN 0-941483-07-X   8.95

DREAMS AND SWORDS by Katherine V. Forrest. 192 pp.
Romantic, erotic, imaginative stories.   ISBN 0-941483-03-7   8.95

MEMORY BOARD by Jane Rule. 336 pp. Memorable novel
about an aging Lesbian couple.   ISBN 0-941483-02-9   9.95

THE ALWAYS ANONYMOUS BEAST by Lauren Wright
Douglas. 224 pp. A Caitlin Reece mystery. First in a series.
                                                 ISBN 0-941483-04-5   8.95

SEARCHING FOR SPRING by Patricia A. Murphy. 224 pp.
Novel about the recovery of love.   ISBN 0-941483-00-2   8.95

DUSTY'S QUEEN OF HEARTS DINER by Lee Lynch. 240 pp.
Romantic blue-collar novel.   ISBN 0-941483-01-0   8.95

PARENTS MATTER by Ann Muller. 240 pp. Parents'
relationships with Lesbian daughters and gay sons.
                                                 ISBN 0-930044-91-6   9.95

THE PEARLS by Shelley Smith. 176 pp. Passion and fun in
the Caribbean sun.   ISBN 0-930044-93-2   7.95

MAGDALENA by Sarah Aldridge. 352 pp. Epic Lesbian novel
set on three continents.   ISBN 0-930044-99-1   8.95

THE BLACK AND WHITE OF IT by Ann Allen Shockley.
144 pp. Short stories.   ISBN 0-930044-96-7   7.95

SAY JESUS AND COME TO ME by Ann Allen Shockley. 288
pp. Contemporary romance.   ISBN 0-930044-98-3   8.95

LOVING HER by Ann Allen Shockley. 192 pp. Romantic love
story. ISBN 0-930044-97-5   7.95

MURDER AT THE NIGHTWOOD BAR by Katherine V.
Forrest. 240 pp. A Kate Delafield mystery. Second in a series.
ISBN 0-930044-92-4   9.95

ZOE'S BOOK by Gail Pass. 224 pp. Passionate, obsessive love
story. ISBN 0-930044-95-9   7.95

WINGED DANCER by Camarin Grae. 228 pp. Erotic Lesbian
adventure story. ISBN 0-930044-88-6   8.95

PAZ by Camarin Grae. 336 pp. Romantic Lesbian adventurer
with the power to change the world. ISBN 0-930044-89-4   8.95

SOUL SNATCHER by Camarin Grae. 224 pp. A puzzle, an
adventure, a mystery — Lesbian romance. ISBN 0-930044-90-8   8.95

THE LOVE OF GOOD WOMEN by Isabel Miller. 224 pp.
Long-awaited new novel by the author of the beloved *Patience
and Sarah.* ISBN 0-930044-81-9   8.95

THE HOUSE AT PELHAM FALLS by Brenda Weathers. 240
pp. Suspenseful Lesbian ghost story. ISBN 0-930044-79-7   7.95

HOME IN YOUR HANDS by Lee Lynch. 240 pp. More stories
from the author of *Old Dyke Tales.* ISBN 0-930044-80-0   7.95

EACH HAND A MAP by Anita Skeen. 112 pp. Real-life poems
that touch us all. ISBN 0-930044-82-7   6.95

SURPLUS by Sylvia Stevenson. 342 pp. A classic early Lesbian
novel. ISBN 0-930044-78-9   7.95

PEMBROKE PARK by Michelle Martin. 256 pp. Derring-do
and daring romance in Regency England. ISBN 0-930044-77-0   7.95

THE LONG TRAIL by Penny Hayes. 248 pp. Vivid adventures
of two women in love in the old west. ISBN 0-930044-76-2   8.95

HORIZON OF THE HEART by Shelley Smith. 192 pp. Hot
romance in summertime New England. ISBN 0-930044-75-4   7.95

AN EMERGENCE OF GREEN by Katherine V. Forrest. 288
pp. Powerful novel of sexual discovery. ISBN 0-930044-69-X   9.95

THE LESBIAN PERIODICALS INDEX edited by Claire
Potter. 432 pp. Author & subject index. ISBN 0-930044-74-6   29.95

DESERT OF THE HEART by Jane Rule. 224 pp. A classic;
basis for the movie *Desert Hearts.* ISBN 0-930044-73-8   9.95

SPRING FORWARD/FALL BACK by Sheila Ortiz Taylor.
288 pp. Literary novel of timeless love. ISBN 0-930044-70-3   7.95

FOR KEEPS by Elisabeth Nonas. 144 pp. Contemporary novel
about losing and finding love. ISBN 0-930044-71-1   7.95

TORCHLIGHT TO VALHALLA by Gale Wilhelm. 128 pp.
Classic novel by a great Lesbian writer. ISBN 0-930044-68-1   7.95

LESBIAN NUNS: BREAKING SILENCE edited by Rosemary
Curb and Nancy Manahan. 432 pp. Unprecedented autobiographies
of religious life.   ISBN 0-930044-62-2   9.95

THE SWASHBUCKLER by Lee Lynch. 288 pp. Colorful novel
set in Greenwich Village in the sixties.   ISBN 0-930044-66-5   8.95

MISFORTUNE'S FRIEND by Sarah Aldridge. 320 pp. Historical Lesbian novel set on two continents.   ISBN 0-930044-67-3   7.95

A STUDIO OF ONE'S OWN by Ann Stokes. Edited by
Dolores Klaich. 128 pp. Autobiography.   ISBN 0-930044-64-9   7.95

SEX VARIANT WOMEN IN LITERATURE by Jeannette
Howard Foster. 448 pp. Literary history.   ISBN 0-930044-65-7   8.95

A HOT-EYED MODERATE by Jane Rule. 252 pp. Hard-hitting
essays on gay life; writing; art.   ISBN 0-930044-57-6   7.95

INLAND PASSAGE AND OTHER STORIES by Jane Rule.
288 pp. Wide-ranging new collection.   ISBN 0-930044-56-8   7.95

WE TOO ARE DRIFTING by Gale Wilhelm. 128 pp. Timeless
Lesbian novel, a masterpiece.   ISBN 0-930044-61-4   6.95

AMATEUR CITY by Katherine V. Forrest. 224 pp. A Kate
Delafield mystery. First in a series.   ISBN 0-930044-55-X   9.95

THE SOPHIE HOROWITZ STORY by Sarah Schulman. 176
pp. Engaging novel of madcap intrigue.   ISBN 0-930044-54-1   7.95

THE YOUNG IN ONE ANOTHER'S ARMS by Jane Rule. 224 pp. Classic
Jane Rule.   ISBN 0-930044-53-3   9.95

OLD DYKE TALES by Lee Lynch. 224 pp. Extraordinary
stories of our diverse Lesbian lives.   ISBN 0-930044-51-7   8.95

DAUGHTERS OF A CORAL DAWN by Katherine V. Forrest.
240 pp. Novel set in a Lesbian new world.   ISBN 0-930044-50-9   8.95

AGAINST THE SEASON by Jane Rule. 224 pp. Luminous,
complex novel of interrelationships.   ISBN 0-930044-48-7   8.95

LOVERS IN THE PRESENT AFTERNOON by Kathleen
Fleming. 288 pp. A novel about recovery and growth.
                                    ISBN 0-930044-46-0   8.95

TOOTHPICK HOUSE by Lee Lynch. 264 pp. Love between
two Lesbians of different classes.   ISBN 0-930044-45-2   7.95

MADAME AURORA by Sarah Aldridge. 256 pp. Historical
novel featuring a charismatic "seer."   ISBN 0-930044-44-4   7.95

BLACK LESBIAN IN WHITE AMERICA by Anita Cornwell.
141 pp. Stories, essays, autobiography.   ISBN 0-930044-41-X   7.95

CONTRACT WITH THE WORLD by Jane Rule. 340 pp.
Powerful, panoramic novel of gay life.   ISBN 0-930044-28-2   9.95

MRS. PORTER'S LETTER by Vicki P. McConnell. 224 pp.
The first Nyla Wade mystery.   ISBN 0-930044-29-0   7.95